THE SILENT SHEPHERD

THE SILENT SHEPHERD

THE CARE, COMFORT, AND CORRECTION OF THE HOLY SPIRIT

JOHN MACARTHUR

THE SILENT SHEPHERD
Published by David C Cook
4050 Lee Vance View
Colorado Springs, CO 80918 U.S.A.

David C Cook Distribution Canada
55 Woodslee Avenue, Paris, Ontario, Canada N3L 3E5

David C Cook U.K., Kingsway Communications
Eastbourne, East Sussex BN23 6NT, England

LCCN 2011942709
ISBN 978-0-7814-0673-4
eISBN 978-1-4347-0485-6

First edition published by Victor Books in 1996

The Team: Alex Field, Amy Konyndyk, Jack Campbell, Karen Athen
Cover Design: Nick Lee
Cover Photo: Shutterstock

Printed in the United States of America
Second Edition 2012

1 2 3 4 5 6 7 8 9 10

112911

CONTENTS

INTRODUCTION

Two errors regarding the doctrine of the Holy Spirit have clouded the contemporary church's understanding of His person and ministry. On the one hand, the charismatic movement is obsessed with the Holy Spirit, tending to focus all doctrine and worship on Him exclusively. The danger with an undue stress on the gifts and leading of the Holy Spirit is that personal experience is often elevated over the objective truth of Scripture. On the other hand, many non-charismatics tend to ignore the Holy Spirit altogether. Perhaps weary of the controversy, confusion, and subjectivity of the charismatic movement, too many have responded by going to the opposite extreme. They simply avoid the Holy Spirit in their teaching and study. On top of that, popular evangelicalism as a whole has shifted in recent generations from God-centered ministry to a man-centered approach. Pragmatism rules. The churches are run as businesses. The gospel is often viewed as a product for marketing. Spiritual problems are dealt with by psychological means. In short, man-centered ministry virtually operates as if the Holy Spirit were unnecessary.

Both errors are spiritually debilitating. If we misunderstand the role of the Holy Spirit, or if we ignore the Spirit altogether, how can we comprehend what it is to walk in the Spirit?

Paul chided the Galatians for their lack of dependence on the Holy Spirit: "Are you so foolish? Having begun by the Spirit, are you now being perfected by the flesh?" (Gal. 3:3). As that verse suggests, the Holy Spirit's role is crucial in bringing us to salvation, in empowering us to live our lives in Christ, and in bringing us to ultimate perfection in glory. In other words, the Spirit's work is essential throughout the entire scope of the Christian's experience. Every aspect of Christian living is governed and empowered by the Holy Spirit. We can ill afford either to misconstrue or ignore His role. To do so is to short-circuit our sanctification. That is exactly what happens when believers turn to legalism, charismatic mysticism, and psychology, as they have today.

Concerning the Holy Spirit's vital position in the life of the church, Charles Ryrie wrote the following paragraph, which is as applicable now as it was in the 1960s:

> The solution to the problems of the church today is to solve the individual Christian's problems, and the solution to those problems is a Person—the Holy Spirit. He is the antidote for every error, the power for every weakness, the victory for every defeat, and the answer for every need. And He is available to every believer, for He lives in his heart and life. The answer and the power have already been given us in the indwelling Holy Spirit.[1]

Unfortunately, such realities have not been fully taken to heart by twenty-first-century Christians. While believers think of Christ as the Good Shepherd (John 10), they rarely see the Holy Spirit as fulfilling a shepherding role. But 1 John 3:24 says, "The one who keeps His commandments abides in Him, and He in him. We know by this that He abides in us, by the Spirit whom He has given us." The apostle is speaking of Christ's indwelling, which is made known to us by the Holy Spirit (John 14:17–20). It is therefore reasonable to see the Spirit working with Christ in shepherding us—ever present to encourage us, guide us, enlighten us in all spiritual truth, and to empower us for every good work (John 14:16, 26–27; 16:13). Hence, I have titled this book *The Silent Shepherd*, which implies the quiet, behind-the-scenes, but nevertheless present ministry of the Holy Spirit.

Too many Christians are searching futilely for answers to needless questions. They flock to seminars, devour popular Christian books, visit counselors, seek the latest fad for successful Christian living, or pursue the current ecstatic experience to discover "the secret" of abundant life in Christ. But I contend that the key to such living is *not* a secret. Nor is it a mystery. Scripture contains all the information we will ever need for living fruitful, successful lives. Our problem is not a lack of information, nor a deficiency in spiritual experience. Our problem is that we do not rely sufficiently on the ministry of the Spirit and allow Him to apply the truth with power in our lives. All the seminars and counselors and deeper-life schemes can actually turn out to be counterproductive, since a false means of sanctification is an impotent counterfeit.

I trust that a new look at those scriptural truths will encourage us to apply the Holy Spirit's resources. We will begin with a review of the basic doctrine of the Holy Spirit. Chapter 1 covers what the Bible teaches about the personality, deity, and works of the Holy Spirit. It also examines the various ways the Holy Spirit is depicted in Scripture.

Another aspect of the Holy Spirit's ministry that is in great need of clarification is His role during the Old Testament period. Over the centuries Christians have tended to give most of their attention to the Spirit in the New Testament. As a result, the church has not always had a good grasp on the significance of the Spirit's role in old covenant people and events. In chapter 2 we will indicate that the Holy Spirit operated in five categories during Old Testament times: in creation, in the empowerment of individuals, in the revelation of God's Word, in the regeneration of individuals, and in the sanctification of believers. The Spirit's activity in the Old Testament provides the foundation for understanding His enhanced role under the new covenant. Such an understanding requires insight into the superiorities of the new covenant itself, which are discussed in chapters 3 and 4.

The fullness of the Holy Spirit in the greater excellence of the new covenant is further underscored by Jesus' promise to His disciples at the very end of His earthly ministry, just prior to His ascension:

> Gathering them together, He commanded them not to leave Jerusalem, but to wait for what the Father had promised, "Which," He said, "you heard of from Me; for John baptized with water, but you

> will be baptized with the Holy Spirit not many days from now." (Acts 1:4–5)

This was the final aspect of the promise Jesus had given earlier to His disciples in the upper room. At that time He pledged, "I will ask the Father, and He will give you another Helper, that He may be with you forever; that is the Spirit of truth, whom the world cannot receive, because it does not see Him or know Him, but you know Him because He abides with you and will be in you" (John 14:16–17).

Of course, Jesus' promise in Acts 1:4–5 was gloriously fulfilled in Acts 2 on the day of Pentecost, when the apostles received the baptism of the Holy Spirit. Since this crucial event in the history of the church is vital for us to understand, our focus in chapter 5 will be an analysis of Spirit baptism. This analysis, I trust, will also give us a clear perspective, in view of all the erroneous teaching on the subject, on the place of Spirit baptism within the body of Christ.

In the final chapters I will focus on the joys we can derive from living the Christian life with a full realization of the Holy Spirit's presence within us. I will devote some space to clarifying a common misperception regarding our relationship to the Holy Spirit. Many contemporary evangelicals have adopted the notion that being filled with the Spirit is something extraordinary, not attainable by most average believers. We will see, however, that all Christians can be continuously filled with the Holy Spirit and are commanded to be so.

The Christian life begins and continues by the power of the Holy Spirit, whom God has graciously sent first to awaken us to our need for salvation, then to give us a new birth, and finally to dwell within us to eventually present us flawless when Christ returns. This will be the theme of this book's final chapters. I trust it will become the underlying theme for the entire book, in keeping with the unchanging truth, "'Not by might nor by power, but by My Spirit,' says the Lord of hosts" (Zech. 4:6).

1

THE SILENT SHEPHERD: A PRIMER

When a Christian recites the simple affirmation from the Apostles' Creed, "I believe in the Holy Ghost," he or she is agreeing (at least outwardly) with one of the great, fundamental beliefs of the Christian faith. But as with all the essential doctrinal truths of the Bible, it is not enough simply to agree intellectually with a bare-bones statement. God always wants His children to embrace the truth wholeheartedly, with a clear mental comprehension *and* a fervent, heartfelt commitment to apply the truth to daily living.

Many older works on the Holy Spirit, while excellent resource books, are inadequate when it comes to applying the truths of the doctrine to Christian growth. On the other hand, many of the popular contemporary books on the Holy Spirit are not doctrinal at all. They assume readers have a foundational knowledge about the Spirit and deal exclusively with experiential aspects of "living in the Spirit." There also is another large block of contemporary material on the arismatic perspective, including its unscriptural nd wrong presuppositions.

to provide you with a balanced presentation g an appropriate doctrinal foundation in this chapter with scriptural discussions in subsequent chapters to point you toward personal application of the Holy Spirit's resources. The following summarizes well my burden for what this book would convey:

> Because God in Christ has initiated the Messianic Age with its outpouring of the Spirit, man's relationship to God has been forever changed. No longer can the Law be used as a means of exclusion and oppression of the disenfranchised: Jesus has preached the messianic Gospel of release to the captive, sight to the blind, and good news to the poor; the new law of life has been written on the hearts of men. Thus we must abhor any new legalism which uses the Scripture to exclude and oppress—this is to turn the good news of Christ into "the letter that kills." We must, rather, recognize the "God-breathed" character of Scripture, and the "Spirit that makes alive." Only so will the Scripture be profitable. Conversely, the Spirit cannot be claimed as the mark of an elite, as that which distinguishes and divides. The Gospel of Jesus Christ includes the message that the Holy Spirit has been poured out on all flesh. All abuses of Scripture and the Spirit must hear God's message: "The promise is to those

> who are near, and to those who are afar off, as many as the Lord our God will call."[1]

It is not my purpose for this to be merely another theology handbook about the Holy Spirit. Yet it is important to focus first on elements of the basic doctrine to lay a foundation for our discussions in the remainder of the book.

Personality of the Spirit

The Holy Spirit is a person. He is not a mystical force or metaphysical influence. He is a divine person—the third person of the Trinity—and acknowledging that fact is absolutely essential to an orthodox understanding of who He is.

Personhood has personality traits, and personality includes intellect, emotions, and will. And these attributes are characteristic of the Holy Spirit.

Attributes of the Holy Spirit

First Corinthians 2:10–11 says, "The Spirit searches all things, even the depths of God. For who among men knows the thoughts of a man except the spirit of the man which is in him? Even so the thoughts of God no one knows except the Spirit of God." These assertions assume that the Holy Spirit has infinite *intelligence* and must therefore be a person (see also Isa. 11:2 and Eph. 1:17).

The New Testament also affirms that the Spirit has *feelings*: "Do not grieve the Holy Spirit of God, by whom you were sealed for the day of redemption" (Eph. 4:30). We must understand, first of all, that divine feelings are not like human passions. God's anger, jealousy, hatred, joy, love, sorrow, and wrath are not reactive or passive emotions like the human variety. That is, His feelings do not rise and fall in response to various stimuli. God is both sovereign and unchanging (Mal. 3:6), so the feelings attributed to Him in Scripture are actually sovereign expressions of His eternal purpose and will, not like human passions that ebb and flow in response to circumstances. (When Scripture assigns such passions to God, it is using a figure of speech known as *anthropopathism*—applying human emotions to God, because our understanding and our language are not adequate to convey the full truth.) Nevertheless, these words mean *something*, and to suggest that the Holy Spirit could feel the emotion of being "grieved" would be meaningless if the Holy Spirit were anything but a person.

The Spirit's guiding of Paul in Acts 16:6–11 illustrates that the Holy Spirit has a *will*. He would not allow the apostle to preach in Asia and Bithynia but instead directed him to go to Europe and Macedonia. His will also determines the various ministries of individual believers, because He is "distributing [spiritual gifts] to each one individually just *as He wills*" (1 Cor. 12:11).

Activities of the Holy Spirit

The Bible describes a wide variety of activities of the Holy Spirit that only a person could perform.

The Spirit Calls People for Special Service

"While they were ministering to the Lord and fasting, the Holy Spirit said, 'Set apart for Me Barnabas and Saul for the work to which I have called them'" (Acts 13:2). "So, being sent out by the Holy Spirit, they went down to Seleucia and from there they sailed to Cyprus" (v. 4).

The Spirit Testifies or Witnesses

"When the Helper comes, whom I will send to you from the Father, that is the Spirit of truth who proceeds from the Father, He will testify about Me" (John 15:26). "The Spirit Himself testifies with our spirit that we are children of God" (Rom. 8:16).

The Spirit Intercedes

"In the same way the Spirit also helps our weakness; for we do not know how to pray as we should, but the Spirit Himself intercedes for us with groanings too deep for words" (Rom. 8:26).

In other places Scripture portrays the Holy Spirit as the *recipient* of various actions and attitudes that demonstrate His personhood. Again, these references would make no sense whatsoever if the Spirit were not a person.

The Spirit Can Be Lied To

"But Peter said, 'Ananias, why has Satan filled your heart to lie to the Holy Spirit, and to keep back some of the price of the land?'" (Acts 5:3).

The Spirit Can Be Blasphemed

"Therefore I say to you, any sin and blasphemy shall be forgiven people, but blasphemy against the Spirit shall not be forgiven" (Matt. 12:31).

Relationships of the Holy Spirit

Because the Holy Spirit is a person, it is logical to assume that He will have relationships with other persons. Scripture illustrates this in many ways. Here are a few examples.

He Has a Relationship with the Apostles

"For it seemed good to the Holy Spirit and to us to lay upon you no greater burden than these essentials" (Acts 15:28—from the letter that the Jerusalem Council sent to the Gentiles at the church in Antioch).

He Has a Relationship with All People

He is related to unbelievers, as indicated in John 16:8–11, "And He, when He comes, will convict the world concerning sin and righteousness and judgment; concerning sin, because they do not believe in Me; and concerning righteousness, because I go to the Father and you no longer see Me; and concerning judgment, because the ruler of this world has been judged."

He is related to believers in many ways, all as a result of His indwelling them. First Corinthians 6:19–20 says, "Or do you not know that your body is a temple of the Holy Spirit who is in you, whom you have from God, and that you are not your own? For you have been bought with a price: therefore glorify God in your body."

He Has a Relationship with Jesus Christ

"But when He, the Spirit of truth, comes, He will guide you into all the truth.... He will glorify Me, for He will take of Mine and will disclose it to you. All things that the Father has are Mine; therefore I said that He takes of Mine and will disclose it to you" (John 16:13–15).

He Is Related to God

"The grace of the Lord Jesus Christ, and the love of God, and the fellowship of the Holy Spirit, be with you all" (2 Cor. 13:14).

The Deity of the Holy Spirit

More than a dozen times in Scripture the Spirit is linked by name and nature to the other two persons of the Trinity (see Matt. 3:16; Acts 16:7; Rom. 8:9; 1 Cor. 2:11; 3:16; 1 Peter 1:11). By various references that ascribe God's attributes to the Holy Spirit, God's Word also demonstrates that the Spirit is God.

The Spirit Possesses Omniscience

"For who among men knows the thoughts of a man except the spirit of the man which is in him? Even so the thoughts of God no one knows except the Spirit of God" (1 Cor. 2:11).

The Spirit Possesses Omnipresence

"Where can I go from Your Spirit? Or where can I flee from Your presence? If I ascend to heaven, You are there; if I make my bed in Sheol, behold, You are there. If I take the wings of the dawn, if I dwell in the remotest part of the sea, even there Your hand will lead me, and Your right hand will lay hold of me" (Ps. 139:7–10).

The Spirit Possesses Omnipotence

"The Spirit of God has made me, and the breath of the Almighty gives me life" (Job 33:4).

The Spirit Is Truth

"It is the Spirit who testifies, because the Spirit is the truth" (1 John 5:6).

The Spirit Possesses Wisdom

"Who has directed the Spirit of the LORD, or as His counselor has informed Him?" (Isa. 40:13).

Works of the Holy Spirit

Even before the contemporary age of specialization, people commonly understood that certain tasks required special materials, tools, and expertise. Only a locksmith could fashion the right replacement key to open a locked hope chest. Only a watchmaker could repair the intricate insides of a pocket watch. Today, only those with specialized knowledge can write software programs for computers. Certain skilled projects have always, by their nature, borne the imprint of experts. This same principle is true on a far more significant level concerning the crucial activities assigned by Scripture to the Holy Spirit. These works, because only one who is God could have performed them, further prove that the Spirit is deity.

The first major work attributed to the Holy Spirit is mentioned in the very first chapter of the Bible: "In the beginning God created the heavens and the earth. The earth was formless and void, and darkness was over the surface of the deep, and the Spirit of God was moving over the surface of the waters" (Gen. 1:1–2). These well-known first verses of Scripture clearly state that the *work of divine creation* was superintended by the Spirit.

Two other familiar verses verify that the Holy Spirit was at work in the *work of Scripture inspiration*: "All Scripture is inspired by God and profitable for teaching, for reproof, for correction, for training in righteousness" (2 Tim. 3:16). "But know this first of all, that no prophecy of Scripture is a matter of one's own interpretation, for no prophecy was ever made by an act of human will, but men moved by the Holy Spirit spoke from God" (2 Peter 1:20–21).

A third major event credited to the Holy Spirit involves the birth of the Lord Jesus. The Spirit's role in the *work of begetting Christ* is presented in the first chapter of the gospel of Luke: "Mary said to the angel, 'How can this be, since I am a virgin?' The angel answered and said to her, 'The Holy Spirit will come upon you, and the power of the Most High will overshadow you; and for that reason the holy Child shall be called the Son of God'" (Luke 1:34–35).

Several other activities of the Holy Spirit—or what more precisely might be called ongoing ministries—are worthy of inclusion as we round out our picture of the Spirit. (We will elaborate on some of these Spirit-directed ministries in later chapters.)

The Spirit Regenerates

"Jesus answered, 'Truly, truly, I say to you, unless one is born of water and the Spirit he cannot enter into the kingdom of God. That which is born of the flesh is flesh, and that which is born of the Spirit is spirit. Do not be amazed that I said to you, "You must be born again." The wind blows where it wishes and you hear the sound of it, but do not know where it comes from and where it is going; so is everyone who is born of the Spirit'" (John 3:5–8).

The Spirit Comforts

"So the church throughout all Judea and Galilee and Samaria enjoyed peace, being built up; and going on in the fear of the Lord and in the comfort of the Holy Spirit, it continued to increase" (Acts 9:31; see also John 14:16, 26; 15:26; 16:7).

The Spirit Sanctifies

"But we should always give thanks to God for you, brethren beloved by the Lord, because God has chosen you from the beginning for salvation through sanctification by the Spirit and faith in the truth" (2 Thess. 2:13).

Representations of the Holy Spirit

We are all familiar with symbols being used to communicate messages or help describe complex concepts. Radio and television with their ever-present, repetitive commercial messages are prime examples of the use of symbols to communicate. For instance, a well-known brand of batteries uses a pink, drum-playing bunny to proclaim the great longevity of those batteries. The bunny has been seen in so many commercials during the past many years that it has become synonymous with the particular brand of battery.

Large companies have used other more abstract symbols for years as trademarks. The Rock of Gibraltar has been used by one of the large insurance companies, and an oval enclosing a sphere (the lens or "eye" of the television camera) has been the corporate emblem of a major TV network.

Long before most man-made symbols were used to represent and promote worldly enterprises, God used figurative language and symbols in the pages of Scripture to convey spiritual truth. The entire Old Testament sacrificial system, with tabernacle and temple, utilized many symbolic items and rituals. The writers of the Psalms, Proverbs, and other poetic books used a lot of figurative and descriptive language to put forth God's truths. Of course, Jesus in His earthly ministry used parables and object lessons to set forth and explain doctrinal concepts. He always used familiar things and ideas that His listeners could identify with.

In a similar manner, God also used analogies to describe the person and work of the Holy Spirit. As long as we don't allegorize or stretch these analogies beyond reasonable limits, the use of symbols and illustrations can help a great deal in understanding who the Spirit is and what He is doing.

The New Testament uses several images to portray the Holy Spirit. They are listed below, along with pertinent Scripture references, roughly in order of importance and familiarity.

The Spirit Portrayed as a Dove

"Now when all the people were baptized, Jesus was also baptized, and while He was praying, heaven was opened, and the Holy Spirit descended upon Him in bodily form like a dove, and a voice came out of heaven, 'You are My beloved Son, in You I am well-pleased'" (Luke 3:21–22; see also Matt. 3:16; Mark 1:10; John 1:32). In this context, the representation of a dove brings to mind the Holy Spirit's purity (see Matt. 10:16, "Be … innocent [pure] as doves"), His heavenly origin, and peace (He rested on Jesus).

The Spirit Portrayed as Fire

"And there appeared to them tongues as of fire distributing themselves, and they rested on each one of them" (Acts 2:3). The little phrase "as of" indicates the tongues were not literal fire but simply suggestive of fire's effect. There was precedence in the Old Testament for the usage of fire in relation to the Lord's presence and works (see Ex. 3:2; 13:21; Lev. 9:24; 10:2; Isa. 6:1–8).

The Spirit Portrayed as Wind

"When the day of Pentecost had come, they were all together in one place. And suddenly there came from heaven a noise like a violent rushing wind, and it filled the whole house where they were sitting" (Acts 2:1–2). Most commentators are agreed that this wind was probably not a literal gust of air that could be felt. As with the tongues of fire, the emphasis is on the vivid word picture used to describe the sound of the Holy Spirit's approaching. So the disciples probably heard the sound of wind but did not necessarily feel a gust. (See also John 3:8, which uses the analogy of the wind in describing the Spirit's sovereign work in regeneration. The verse is probably also an allusion to Ezekiel 37:9–14, where the prophet commands the wind to breathe life into the dead bodies.)

The Spirit Portrayed as One Who Seals

"In Him, you also, after listening to the message of truth, the gospel of your salvation—having also believed, you were sealed in Him with the Holy Spirit of promise" (Eph. 1:13; see also 2 Cor. 1:22; Eph. 4:30). This sealing refers to the mark or token of ownership that completed a transaction. (For a fuller discussion of the Holy Spirit as a seal, see my commentary on Ephesians in *The MacArthur New Testament Commentary*.)

The Spirit Portrayed as a Pledge

"Now He who prepared us for this very purpose is God, who gave to us the Spirit as a pledge" (2 Cor. 5:5; see also 1:22; Eph. 1:14). Most of us are familiar with the concept of earnest money or a down payment in connection with a major purchase. By making a down payment, we pledge to complete the transaction. God's gift of the Spirit to us is His verification to us that our salvation will be completed in glorification. It is His promise to give us all the future blessings of that salvation.

The Spirit Portrayed as Water

"Now on the last day, the great day of the feast, Jesus stood and cried out, saying, 'If anyone is thirsty, let him come to Me and drink. He who believes in Me, as the Scripture said, "From his innermost being will flow rivers of living water."' But this He spoke of the Spirit, whom those who believed in Him were to receive; for the Spirit was not yet given, because Jesus was not yet glorified" (John 7:37–39). Several references in the Old Testament also compare the Holy Spirit to water and are strongly suggestive that water revived that which was barren or dead (Isa. 32:15; 44:3; Joel 2:28–29).

The Spirit Portrayed as Clothing

"And behold, I am sending forth the promise of My Father upon you; but you are to stay in the city until you are clothed with power from on high" (Luke 24:49). In this verse Jesus was clearly using "promise" and "power" to refer to the Holy Spirit. Therefore the clothing image also relates to the Spirit, and its significance is fairly plain. Just as clothing covers and protects us, so does the Holy Spirit. Just as special clothing (uniforms, academic robes) signifies certain relationships, so the Spirit shows that we belong to God. (See also the illustration of the Prodigal Son and his robe in Luke 15:22.)

In this short primer on the identity of the Holy Spirit, we have been reminded that He has divine attributes as the third person of the Trinity. As a member of the Godhead, the Spirit has His own unique, vital, and indispensable role to perform in the creation and nurturing of the true church. We see that the Holy Spirit has been working and ministering throughout all eternity. Even though the Spirit becomes more prominent in the new covenant age, that does not mean He was inactive during old covenant times. This truth will become clearer as we look in more detail at the role of the Holy Spirit in the Old Testament in chapter 2.

2

THE SPIRIT IN THE OLD TESTAMENT

How information is distributed, received, and interpreted determines the clarity with which it is understood. This principle was illustrated quite vividly for millions of American radio listeners on October 30, 1938, a date that has since been referred to by many historians as "the night that panicked America." A twenty-three-year-old genius writer, producer, and actor named Orson Welles presented a nation-wide audience with a dramatic adaptation of the H. G. Wells science fiction novel *War of the Worlds*, which describes an invasion of earth by machine-like creatures from Mars.

Welles' drama was presented on a weekly anthology program, *The Mercury Theatre*, which usually dramatized a classic play or book. Welles and his fellow actors presented *War of the Worlds* as if it were special news coverage of actual events. They offered a disclaimer at the beginning of the program and several times during the broadcast to inform listeners that they were hearing a drama, not a real newscast. However, many people tuned in after the program started or somehow failed to recognize the disclaimers during the course of the program. As a result, thousands of people thought the broadcast was describing the start of a real invasion from Mars. Many tried to flee by car from New York City, which caused massive, chaotic traffic jams on the highways leading out of the metropolitan area. (The radio drama portrayed the Martian invasion as beginning in rural New Jersey and heading for New York and other major cities.)

The following day an embarrassed Orson Welles sheepishly made a public apology for frightening the American people. No doubt many of them also were embarrassed for believing the program was a description of actual events. The entire episode has ever since been a classic case study in how misinformation or "missed information" can result in widespread panic.

Seldom does miscommunication of biblical or doctrinal truth lead so quickly to erroneous thinking or overt confusion. The effect is usually more gradual and long-term, but far more damaging. And any mishandling of God's Word does far more harm simply because the Word is concerned with more profound issues—those things that really matter in the Christian life.

Two Spirits or One?

My chief burden in this book is to communicate a clear and accurate understanding of the Holy Spirit, our Silent Shepherd. This implies that we might need to correct our previous thinking in some areas. One of these areas is our understanding of the Holy

Spirit's work in the Old Testament. Are there similarities and continuities between the old covenant and the new concerning the Spirit's role? Or are there such vast differences that we, in effect, have to see two completely different manifestations of the Spirit—one in the Old Testament and a completely different one in the New?

In answering these questions, it is crucial that we bear in mind that there is only one Spirit and that He is God and is therefore immutable (unchanging). Paul wrote,

- "But one and the same Spirit works all these things [bestowing of various spiritual gifts], distributing to each one individually just as He wills" (1 Cor. 12:11).

- "For by one Spirit we were all baptized into one body, whether Jews or Greeks, whether slaves or free, and we were all made to drink of one Spirit" (1 Cor. 12:13).

- "There is one body and one Spirit, just as also you were called in one hope of your calling" (Eph. 4:4).

Paul was referring to the Holy Spirit's work among New Testament believers. However, the emphasis is quite clear that there is *one* Spirit. The *same* eternal Spirit was at work during the Old and New Testament periods. The Holy Spirit was, is, and always will be the saving agent who draws people to the Lord. If there were not such a strong continuity in the Spirit's saving ministry, Jesus would not have taught Nicodemus as He did:

> Jesus answered, "Truly, truly, I say to you, unless one is born of water and the Spirit he cannot enter into the kingdom of God. That which is born of the flesh is flesh, and that which is born of the Spirit is spirit. Do not be amazed that I said to you, 'You must be born again.' The wind blows where it wishes and you hear the sound of it, but do not know where it comes from and where it is going; so is everyone who is born of the Spirit."
>
> Nicodemus said to Him, "How can these things be?" Jesus answered and said to him, "Are you the teacher of Israel and do not understand these things?" (John 3:5–10)

This brief passage ends with Jesus in effect reprimanding Nicodemus, a Jewish religious leader, for not knowing the Old Testament better. As one who supposedly knew God's law, Nicodemus should not have been so baffled by Jesus' explanation of the new birth and the Holy Spirit's role in it. (Jesus met with Nicodemus before the new covenant was ratified at the cross, so our Lord's salvation instruction was based on Old Testament truths.)

So there is certainly much continuity in the Holy Spirit's work between the Old and New Testaments.

Nevertheless, careful study and interpretation of the whole of Scripture reveals that there are also *distinctions* between the old covenant and the new covenant concerning the Spirit's role. What occurred at Pentecost, for example, is described as a new baptism of the Spirit (Acts 1:5). It is His role that differs, however, not the essential character of the Spirit Himself. His enhanced role under the new covenant is more intimate, more personal—but still similar in character to the way we see Him functioning in the Old Testament.

There is no need to be ignorant or confused about the Holy Spirit's place in the overall scope of redemptive history—from Genesis 1:1 to the prophets to Jesus' earthly ministry to the early church, right down to the present.

The Spirit in Creation

The first important role the Old Testament ascribes to the Holy Spirit concerns His involvement in creation. Genesis 1:1–2 says, "In the beginning God created the heavens and the earth. The earth was formless and void, and darkness was over the surface of the deep, and the Spirit of God was moving over the surface of the waters." First of all, God the Father, through Jesus Christ the Son, out of nothing created the substance of the universe. (This is what theologians call *ex nihilo* creation, the essence of which is expressed in John 1:3.) Then the Holy Spirit, as the third person of the Trinity, was charged with the task of overseeing the creation of matter, energy, and all plant life, animal life, and human life.

Old Testament scholar Edward J. Young explained the meaning of the phrase "moving over the surface of the waters" in Genesis 1:2 this way: "It is to be translated 'hovering,' and the picture is that of the Spirit of God hovering over all things as a bird hovers over its nest, so that the Spirit of God is holding all things in control."[1]

The prophet Isaiah, through a series of rhetorical questions, described the power and self-sufficiency of the Holy Spirit in the creation:

> Who has measured the waters in the hollow of His hand, and marked off the heavens by the span, and calculated the dust of the earth by the measure, and weighed the mountains in a balance and the hills in a pair of scales? Who has directed the Spirit of the LORD, or as His counselor has informed Him? With whom did He consult and who gave Him understanding? And who taught Him in the path of justice and taught Him knowledge and informed Him of the way of understanding? (Isa. 40:12–14)

The Spirit's power is illustrated rather obviously in the picturesque language of verse 12, which is only a partial listing of His marvelous work in bringing order out of the formless substance that the Father created through the Son.

Job 33:4 also affirms the Holy Spirit's role in the creation. Here Elihu, one of Job's friends, testified to the truth that the Spirit created humankind: "The Spirit of God has made me, and the breath of the Almighty gives me life."

Empowered by the Spirit

The second major activity of the Holy Spirit in the Old Testament is empowerment. By empowerment I mean the action by which people are enabled or equipped for the accomplishment of special, divinely designed tasks. These were tasks that required ability beyond the normal, beyond what people could do on their own. We can see this in many specific places in the Old Testament, marked by the expression "the Spirit of the Lord came upon ..." The same concept of empowerment was implicit concerning God's call of Abraham (Gen. 12:1–3) and Moses (Ex. 3:14), even if that formula expression was not used.

The Old Testament has four main categories of people who experienced empowerment by the Holy Spirit.

The Judges

The first category of Old Testament people empowered by the Spirit is the judges. The book of Judges covered a crucial transition period in Israel's history, between Joshua and Samuel, when the nation endured a series of spiritual declensions during which the nation's neighbors oppressed it. In Judges the writer makes repeated references "to the fact that the Spirit of God came upon men supernaturally gifted, and who were raised up for the deliverance of Israel."[2] These gifted men included Othniel (Judg. 3:9), Gideon (6:34), Jephthah (11:29), Samson (14—16)—four of the most prominent judges. (Samuel, often called the last judge of Israel, did not appear until 1 Samuel.)

Nineteenth-century Scottish theologian George Smeaton, a contemporary of Robert Murray McCheyne and Andrew Bonar, summarized what happened each time the Holy Spirit specially selected a judge to rescue Israel:

> The Spirit of God, the author of all those gifts which they received, intellectual as well as spiritual, kindled in them intrepid valour; for God was King of the Theocracy, and it redounded to His glory to break the yoke of the oppressor, when the purposes

> of discipline were served. One hero after another, endowed with extraordinary courage, patriotism, and zeal, was raised up by the Spirit of God to deliver Israel.[3]

Thus it is clear that the judges were not self-made men or routine heroes. They made a significant, supernatural impact only because they were energized by God's Spirit.

Craftsmen

Special craftsmen were also empowered by the Holy Spirit in the Old Testament. The best-known example is Bezalel, who was the chief artisan in the construction of the tabernacle. Exodus 31:1–11 introduces Bezalel and his associate Oholiab this way:

> Now the LORD spoke to Moses, saying, "See, I have called by name Bezalel, the son of Uri, the son of Hur, of the tribe of Judah. I have filled him with the Spirit of God in wisdom, in understanding, in knowledge, and in all kinds of craftsmanship, to make artistic designs for work in gold, in silver, and in bronze, and in the cutting of stones for settings, and in the carving of wood, that he may work in all kinds of craftsmanship. And behold, I Myself have appointed with him Oholiab, the son of Ahisamach, of the tribe of Dan; and in the hearts of all who are skillful I have put skill, that they may make all that I have commanded you: the tent of meeting, and

> the ark of testimony, and the mercy seat upon it, and all the furniture of the tent, the table also and its utensils, and the pure gold lampstand with all its utensils, and the altar of incense, the altar of burnt offering also with all its utensils, and the laver and its stand, the woven garments as well, and the holy garments for Aaron the priest, and the garments of his sons, with which to carry on their priesthood; the anointing oil also, and the fragrant incense for the holy place, they are to make them according to all that I have commanded you."

This passage outlines the great array of craftsmanship Bezalel had charge of (see also Ex. 35:30—36:2; 37:1ff.). All the items he and his associates built were related to the worship of God and were achieved with special aid of the Holy Spirit, who enabled them to do the work as God prescribed it.

National Leaders

God saw fit to send His Spirit upon some Old Testament men to empower them for national leadership. David was one such leader. God selected him to be Israel's king after Saul's failure. The Lord worked through Samuel, who himself had been empowered by God's Spirit as the last of Israel's judges:

> Now the LORD said to Samuel, "How long will you grieve over Saul, since I have rejected him from being king over Israel? Fill your horn with oil

and go; I will send you to Jesse the Bethlehemite, for I have selected a king for Myself among his sons." But Samuel said, "How can I go? When Saul hears of it, he will kill me." And the LORD said, "Take a heifer with you and say, 'I have come to sacrifice to the LORD.' You shall invite Jesse to the sacrifice, and I will show you what you shall do; and you shall anoint for Me the one whom I designate to you." So Samuel did what the LORD said, and came to Bethlehem. And the elders of the city came trembling to meet him and said, "Do you come in peace?" He said, "In peace; I have come to sacrifice to the LORD. Consecrate yourselves and come with me to the sacrifice." He also consecrated Jesse and his sons and invited them to the sacrifice.

When they entered, he looked at Eliab and thought, "Surely the LORD's anointed is before Him." But the LORD said to Samuel, "Do not look at his appearance or at the height of his stature, because I have rejected him; for God sees not as man sees, for man looks at the outward appearance, but the LORD looks at the heart." Then Jesse called Abinadab and made him pass before Samuel. And he said, "The LORD has not chosen this one either." Next Jesse made Shammah pass by. And he said, "The LORD has not chosen this one either." Thus Jesse made seven of his sons pass before Samuel.

> But Samuel said to Jesse, "The LORD has not chosen these." And Samuel said to Jesse, "Are these all the children?" And he said, "There remains yet the youngest, and behold, he is tending the sheep." Then Samuel said to Jesse, "Send and bring him; for we will not sit down until he comes here."
>
> So he sent and brought him in. Now he was ruddy, with beautiful eyes and a handsome appearance. And the LORD said, "Arise, anoint him; for this is he." Then Samuel took the horn of oil and anointed him in the midst of his brothers; and the Spirit of the LORD came mightily upon David from that day forward. And Samuel arose and went to Ramah. (1 Sam. 16:1–13)

From that time on, David occupied a special position within God's program for Israel. But that does not mean he was always submissive to God's will or perfectly obedient to the Holy Spirit's leading. David's sin against Bathsheba and her husband, Uriah (2 Sam. 11), shows that he was far from being a continual role model to his people. David certainly realized this when he prayed the following, which is part of his prayer of contrition in Psalm 51, following the episode with Bathsheba:

> Create in me a clean heart, O God, and renew a steadfast spirit within me. Do not cast me away from Your presence and do not take Your Holy Spirit from me. Restore to me the joy of Your

> salvation and sustain me with a willing spirit. (Ps. 51:10–12)

In this psalm David even urged God not to remove the Holy Spirit from him. David's request brings up an intriguing question concerning the Spirit's role in the Old Testament—a question that has confused many Christians and led them to wrong conclusions. Because of well-known cases such as King Saul (1 Sam. 16:14) and Samson (Judg. 16:20), in which the Spirit of the Lord departed from them, believers have asked two questions: "Is that the normal way the Holy Spirit dealt with all Old Testament people?" and "Does having the Spirit removed mean people could lose their salvation?"

The answer to that twofold question is a resounding no! The Old Testament writers never intended to portray Samson and Saul as typical examples for believers. First, the granting and withdrawing of the Spirit was related to the special kinds of empowerment we have discussed in this section. In David's case it had nothing to do with his personal relationship to God but with his desire to keep the unique spiritual anointing that made him an effective king on God's behalf. Second, the concept of losing one's salvation is incompatible with the New Testament's basic teaching on the security of salvation (John 6:37–40; 10:27–30) and the Spirit's role in securing it (Rom. 8:9, 16–17; Eph. 1:13–14).

Salvation is the same in every era, so it would be wrong to link the increasing and decreasing manifestations of the Holy Spirit's power in the Old Testament with the Spirit's saving work and therefore see Old Testament believers as losing their salvation.

The Prophets

The final category of Old Testament figures empowered by the Holy Spirit for a special purpose is the prophets. The Spirit's empowerment of them was related to the task of conveying God's revealed word to His people. *The Evangelical Dictionary of Theology* defines *prophet* and describes the prophet's function as follows:

> The word "prophet" comes from the Greek *prophetes*, from *pro* ("before" or "for") and *phemi* ("to speak"). The prophet is thus the one who speaks before in the sense of proclaim, or the one who speaks for, i.e., in the name of (God).... The originality of biblical prophecy derives from the phenomenon of inspiration. As distinct from the sacral figures of pagan antiquity the biblical prophet is not a magician. He does not force God. On the contrary, he is under divine constraint. It is God who invites, summons, and impels him—e.g., Jer. 20:7.[4]

Many examples of this unique, divine empowerment can be drawn from the prophets of the Old Testament period, but two illustrative verses (one from a major prophet, one from a minor prophet) will be adequate. Ezekiel 11:5 says, "Then the Spirit of the LORD fell upon me, and He said to me, 'Say, "Thus says the LORD, 'So you think, house of Israel, for I know your thoughts.'""" Micah 3:8 adds this statement: "On the other hand I am filled with power—with the Spirit of the LORD—and with justice and courage to make known to Jacob his rebellious act, even to Israel his sin."

This brief survey of the Holy Spirit's fourfold ministry of empowerment eliminates the common misperceptions regarding His supposed absence or inactivity during the Old Testament period. Each aspect of empowerment, from the pragmatic results produced by the tabernacle craftsmen to the profound, lasting effects of the prophets' words, demonstrates that the Holy Spirit played a prolific and significant role throughout the old covenant.

Revelation by the Spirit

The Holy Spirit's third area of ministry in Old Testament times—the revelation of divine truth by divine words—flows smoothly and logically from our previous discussion of prophetic empowerment. The writer of Hebrews started his letter with these words: "God, after He spoke long ago to the fathers in the prophets in many portions and in many ways" (Heb. 1:1). F. F. Bruce said, "The earlier stage of the revelation [Old Testament] was given in a variety of ways: God spoke in His mighty works of mercy and judgment; and made known through His servants the prophets the meaning and purpose of these works; they were admitted into His secret council and learned His plans in advance. He spoke in storm and thunder to Moses, in a still small voice to Elijah."[5]

The Holy Spirit was not simply present and occasionally intervening in Old Testament events. He was and is the author of the Old Testament books that we read today. This great truth derives directly from the apostle Paul's classic statement in 2 Timothy 3:16: "All Scripture is inspired by God." When Paul wrote that, the "all Scripture" he referred to was the Old Testament. Therefore it is obvious that the Holy Spirit would have been active and involved in revealing God's Word to the writers of the Old Testament.

The phrase "is inspired by God" is a translation of the theologically important Greek word *theopneustos*, which literally means "God-breathed." The very use of this term, with the root *pneustos* closely related to *pneuma*, "spirit," strongly implies the Holy Spirit was involved in the entire process of revealing God's Word. Every thought and sentence of the Old as well as the New Testament is the breathed-out Word of God, which was faithfully recorded by the Spirit-guided writers.

The words of the apostle Peter provide us with additional New Testament verification that the Holy Spirit was at work revealing the Old Testament Scripture to Moses, the prophets, and all the other godly writers: "But know this first of all, that no prophecy of Scripture is a matter of one's own interpretation, for no prophecy was ever made by an act of human will, but men moved by the Holy Spirit spoke from God" (2 Peter 1:20–21).

In the Old Testament itself, the men God used to write Scripture testify to the Holy Spirit's role in that process:

- "Now these are the last words of David. David the son of Jesse declares, the man who was raised on high declares, the anointed of the God of Jacob, and the sweet psalmist of Israel, 'The Spirit of the LORD spoke by me, and His word was on my tongue'" (2 Sam. 23:1–2).

- "However, You [God] bore with them for many years, and admonished them by Your Spirit through Your prophets" (Neh. 9:30).

- "They made their hearts like flint so that they could not hear the law and the words which the LORD of hosts had sent by His Spirit through the former prophets" (Zech. 7:12).

Regeneration by the Spirit

The fourth major ministry of the Holy Spirit in the Old Testament was the regeneration of sinners. Earlier in this chapter we noted that Jesus chided Nicodemus for his ignorance of the Spirit's role in regeneration (John 3:10). Clearly the Holy Spirit was vitally involved in the regeneration of people during Old Testament times.

Theologian J. I. Packer provided the following concise overview of regeneration in the Old Testament:

> In OT prophecies regeneration is depicted as the work of God renovating, circumcising, and softening Israelite hearts, writing His laws upon them, and thereby causing their owners to know, love, and obey Him as never before (Deut. 30:6; Jer. 31:31-34; 32:39-40; Ezek. 11:19-20; 36:25-27). It is a sovereign work of purification from sin's defilement (Ezek. 36:25; see also Ps. 51:10), wrought by the personal energy of God's creative outbreathing ("spirit": Ezek. 36:27; 39:29). Jeremiah declares that such renovation on a national scale will introduce and signal God's new

> messianic administration of His covenant with His people (Jer. 31:31; 32:40).[6]

An integral part of the work of regeneration is the prior conviction of sin. Conviction by the Holy Spirit is not just a New Testament concept. The Spirit's work of conviction is recorded on the beginning pages of the Old Testament: "Then the LORD said, 'My Spirit shall not strive with man forever, because he also is flesh'" (Gen. 6:3). That statement looks ahead to what Jesus would teach His disciples in the upper room: "And He [the Holy Spirit], when He comes, will convict the world concerning sin and righteousness and judgment" (John 16:8). Once again there is a clear continuity between the Old and New Testaments regarding what the Holy Spirit does.

The early operation of the Holy Spirit's convicting ministry also proves the reality of humankind's total depravity since the fall. Many people are confused by the term *total depravity*. It does not mean that all people are as evil as they can possibly be. It means that the principle of sin has pervaded every aspect of human nature. We are corrupted through and through with sin. Even though the expression of sin might not individually be as thoroughly evil as humanity is capable of, we are totally and thoroughly depraved and utterly incapable of any good that would merit salvation. Our wills are bent inexorably toward evil. Given choices, we will inevitably sin, rebel against God, and destroy ourselves spiritually. And we can do nothing to change our nature or relationship of enmity against God. That's total depravity.

Because total depravity came with the fall, we know it affected Old Testament people and everyone since. In fact, before the flood,

Scripture tells us, "The LORD saw that the wickedness of man was great on the earth, and that every intent of the thoughts of his heart was only evil continually" (Gen. 6:5). Things were no different after the deluge, however. God said, "The intent of man's heart is evil from his youth" (8:21). Total depravity still tainted the human race—and does to this day. Jeremiah said, "The heart is deceitful above all things, and desperately wicked" (Jer. 17:9 KJV).

Consider the description of depravity in Romans 3:10–18:

> There is none righteous, not even one; there is none who understands, there is none who seeks for God; all have turned aside, together they have become useless; there is none who does good, there is not even one. Their throat is an open grave, with their tongues they keep deceiving, the poison of asps is under their lips; whose mouth is full of cursing and bitterness; their feet are swift to shed blood, destruction and misery are in their paths, and the path of peace they have not known. There is no fear of God before their eyes.

Paul's entire thought in this passage is derived from the following Old Testament verses: Psalms 5:9; 10:7; 14:1–3; 36:1; 53:1–4; 140:3; and Isaiah 59:7ff. His usage of these verses again emphasizes that our depravity and our need for the Holy Spirit in conviction and regeneration are teachings rooted in the Old Testament. Therefore, all Old Testament believers were born again as a result of the Spirit's miraculous work in their hearts, not by any other method (Deut. 30:6; see also Jer. 13:23; 31:31–34; Ezek. 36:25–27; 37:5–6).

Hebrews 11 is an additional New Testament tribute to the Holy Spirit's Old Testament ministry of regeneration. The writer of Hebrews rightly assumed throughout the chapter that all the Old Testament role models, from Abel to the last of the prophets, were genuine believers. There is no way any of them could have lived such exemplary lives of faith without being regenerated by the Holy Spirit. Because the theology of regeneration was not fully defined until Jesus' time does not make it any less a reality for the old covenant believers.

To illustrate that, we can draw an analogy from the weather. In recent decades meteorologists have made great strides in the technology of weather observation, forecasting, storm tracking, and so forth. Photographs from weather satellites show us the locations of developing storms and the movements of clouds and frontal systems. Computers can analyze data and produce five- and ten-day models of how the weather will likely unfold. However, just because such technology did not exist a century ago does not mean the weather was necessarily that different from today's patterns and cycles. Storms still exhibited certain God-given characteristics; we simply couldn't understand or forecast them as well as we do today.

Preservation by the Spirit

The final important ministry of the Holy Spirit in the Old Testament was the preservation of the believer. We have just seen that He graciously and sovereignly regenerated individuals during Old Testament times. It logically follows that, in the lives of those in whom He brought new life, the Spirit would have been busily engaged in the significant ministry of preserving and perfecting.

The New Testament has much to say about the security of the believer, especially John 10:27–29: "My sheep hear My voice, and I know them, and they follow Me; and I give eternal life to them, and they will never perish; and no one will snatch them out of My hand. My Father, who has given them to Me, is greater than all; and no one is able to snatch them out of the Father's hand." John 5:24; 6:37; Romans 5:5; 8:9–17; and Ephesians 1:13–14 are other passages that give assurance of salvation. Even the "Westminster Confession of Faith" says the following: "They, whom God hath accepted in His Beloved, effectually called, and sanctified by His Spirit, can neither totally nor finally fall away from the state of grace, but shall certainly persevere therein to the end, and be eternally saved" (chapter XVII, section I).

A New Testament perspective definitely makes it clear that God, through the Holy Spirit, draws us to Himself and preserves us in that relationship (Rom. 8:29–30, 35–39; Jude vv. 24–25). But we tend to overlook or be unaware of the fact that the Spirit also preserved Old Testament saints in their relationships with God.

Remember what David said in his prayer of contrition in Psalm 51:10–12, after Nathan the prophet had pointed out David's adultery with Bathsheba and murder of her husband:

> Create in me a clean heart, O God, and renew a steadfast spirit within me. Do not cast me away from Your presence and do not take Your Holy

> Spirit from me. Restore to me the joy of Your salvation and sustain me with a willing spirit.

David recognized that to live an obedient and pleasing life as a believer he needed divine help. He was not looking to his own effort and strength to get his life back on track. It is also clear from these verses that David knew he needed the Holy Spirit's empowerment if he was going to continue as leader of Israel. The narrative in 2 Samuel 12 implicitly proves that the Spirit sustained David. He brought David through the discipline of losing his illegitimate child, enabled him to worship God again, gave him a new son (Solomon), and restored him in love (v. 24).

The psalmist (most often David) in numerous places showed his understanding of the Holy Spirit's preserving ministry, perhaps best represented in Psalm 125:1–2: "Those who trust in the LORD are as Mount Zion, which cannot be moved but abides forever. As the mountains surround Jerusalem, so the LORD surrounds His people from this time forth and forever" (see also Pss. 1:3; 34:7; 37:24; 48:14; 66:9; 92:12; 119:33; 138:8).

The Old Testament prophets understood this truth as well. Isaiah said, "But now, thus says the LORD, your Creator, O Jacob, and He who formed you, O Israel, 'Do not fear, for I have redeemed you; I have called you by name; you are Mine! When you pass through the waters, I will be with you; and through the rivers, they will not overflow you. When you walk through the fire, you will not be scorched, nor will the flame burn you'" (Isa. 43:1–2; see also 46:4; 54:10; 59:21). Ezekiel 36:27 gives further support to a preserving ministry by the Spirit: "I will put My Spirit within you and cause you to walk in My statutes, and you will be careful to observe My ordinances." (This verse upholds Paul's teaching in Ephesians 2:10: "For we are His workmanship, created in Christ Jesus for good works, which God prepared beforehand so that we would walk in them." See also Jer. 31:3; 32:40; Ezek. 11:19–20.)

The scriptural evidence overwhelmingly points to a significant Old Testament role for the Holy Spirit. God's Spirit had a vital role in the creation of the world and the revelation of the Old Testament Scripture. He had an equally important part to play in the spiritual lives of the Old Testament elect, in their regeneration and preservation.

I trust the full-orbed nature of the Holy Spirit's ministry will become clearer than ever for you as this study unfolds. In the upcoming chapters we will see distinctions in the Spirit's ministry from the old to the new covenant—there is a greater fullness, richness, and depth of experiencing the Spirit for new covenant believers. But I pray we will be reminded, above all, that the Holy Spirit has been and is at work in every age of God's program, because "There is one body and one Spirit, just as also you were called in one hope of your calling" (Eph. 4:4).

3

THE SPIRIT OF LIFE: THE NEW COVENANT

At the end of the previous chapter's discussion of the Spirit's often-overlooked Old Testament ministries, we noted the Spirit's greater prominence under the fuller revelation of the new covenant. This increased involvement for the Holy Spirit with believers implies more than a superficial difference between the Testaments. The superiority of the New over the Old begins to come into focus. If we are to fully appreciate the Holy Spirit's ministry potential in our lives, it is helpful to study the significance of the new covenant and understand its superlatives.

A Better Covenant

Matthew 26:27–28 says, "And when He had taken a cup and given thanks, He gave it to them, saying, 'Drink from it, all of you; for this is My blood of the covenant, which is poured out for many for forgiveness of sins.'" These are Jesus' own words to His disciples at the Last Supper, the night before His death. This one sentence is filled with extremely important truth about the new covenant. Our Lord provided the basis of the covenant, His blood (or death), and He revealed the distinctive purpose for the covenant: to provide forgiveness of sins.

That is why the new covenant stands in sharp contrast to the old covenant. The new is the essence and epitome of God's redemptive plan. It reveals in clear-cut terms the basis for salvation, whereas the old covenant was laden with symbolism that merely pointed toward the true means of atonement. The sacrifices and symbols of the old covenant could never by themselves save anyone. All the ceremonies, including circumcision, animal sacrifices, and various washings, were merely symbolic. They were shadows, pictures, and types that looked forward to the reality of the new covenant, ratified through the death of Jesus Christ. Simply stated, they were elements of an inferior covenant, and they had no saving efficacy of their own (Heb. 10:4, 11).

The author of the epistle to the Hebrews, inspired and moved by the Holy Spirit, gave an excellent synopsis of the new covenant as the better covenant:

> But now He has obtained a more excellent ministry, by as much as He is also the mediator of a better covenant, which has been enacted on better promises.
>
> For if that first covenant had been faultless, there would have been no occasion sought for a second. For finding fault with them, He says, "Behold, days are coming, says the Lord, when I will effect a new covenant with the house of Israel and with the house

> of Judah; not like the covenant which I made with their fathers on the day when I took them by the hand to lead them out of the land of Egypt; for they did not continue in My covenant, and I did not care for them, says the Lord. For this is the covenant that I will make with the house of Israel after those days, says the Lord: I will put My laws into their minds, and I will write them on their hearts. And I will be their God, and they shall be My people. And they shall not teach everyone his fellow citizen, and everyone his brother, saying, 'Know the Lord,' for all will know Me, from the least to the greatest of them. For I will be merciful to their iniquities, and I will remember their sins no more." When He said, "A new covenant," He has made the first obsolete. But whatever is becoming obsolete and growing old is ready to disappear. (Heb. 8:6–13)

A brief examination of this passage reveals two basic facts about the new covenant: It has a better mediator, Jesus Christ; and it has better characteristics, being based on better promises.

A Better Mediator

Every covenant has a mediator. A mediator is someone who stands between two parties and brings the parties together. To do so, the mediator must represent both sides equally. Because He is fully God and fully man, Jesus Christ is the only person who could be the mediator between God and humanity (1 Tim. 2:5). And He is the better mediator of a better covenant—the new covenant.

Under the old covenant, human priests and human leaders were the visible mediators. Moses, for example, was in a mediatorial role (Ex. 20:19; Deut. 5:5; Gal. 3:19). The Levitical priests also were mediators because they represented the people before God in the sacrifices that were offered. The prophets too were mediators in a certain sense because they brought God's Word to the people. But even though Moses, the priests, and the prophets could all be seen as real mediators, they possessed one major deficiency. None of them could equally represent both sides (God and humanity) because none of them was God. Obviously in order to represent both sides with perfect satisfaction and equality, a mediator would have to be both God and human. And that brings us to 1 Timothy 2:5: "For there is one God, and one mediator also between God and men, the man Christ Jesus." The only perfect mediator who could meet all the qualifications for fair, just, and complete mediation was Jesus Christ, who was both God and man.

Therefore it's clear that the new covenant has a better mediator than the old. None could possibly be better than the Lord Jesus Christ. He is the supreme and perfect mediator whose role was the greater reality that was only pictured and foreshadowed by the work of the Levitical priesthood under the old covenant.

Based on Better Promises

The new covenant also was based on better promises. All covenants, by their very nature, are promises. The old covenant was based on promises between God and Israel, as Moses reminded the people (Deut. 5:1–5). But the promises were woven into the detailed and complex character of the old covenant, with its many sacrifices, rituals, commandments, and lengthy instructions for living. These legal aspects of the old covenant touched upon every conceivable aspect of life—including strict limitations on what the people could eat and wear. The entire system was burdensome, repetitive, and impossible for the people to fulfill. (A basic reading of the related chapters in Exodus, Leviticus, Numbers, and Deuteronomy reveal those old covenant legal characteristics in greater detail.)

Why were so many shadowy, symbolic, legal elements included in the old covenant? It's important to grasp this issue carefully. The old covenant was not "a covenant of works," as some would suggest. Salvation under the old covenant was not obtained by obedience to the law. Even under the old covenant, salvation was by grace through faith, in accordance with the promise of salvation God initially made to Abraham and his seed. The law of Moses did not nullify the promise of salvation by grace through faith God had previously made to Abraham (see Gal. 3:14–17). So even under the old covenant, salvation was offered in the gracious promise God made to Abraham because of the work of Jesus Christ, whom God identified as "the Lamb slain from the foundation of the world" (Rev. 13:8 KJV).

This indicates that His death was the sacrifice that covered Old Testament saints. Because of God's application of the sacrifice of Christ to all believers in the old covenant, the writer of Hebrews wrote, "His works were finished from the foundation of the world" (Heb. 4:3).

That is why the letter to the Hebrews says the promises of the new covenant are superior. For one thing, they are not laden with the repeated sacrifices and ceremonies, "which are a mere shadow of what is to come; but the substance belongs to Christ" (Col. 2:17). The new covenant promises deliver the substance that the shadows of the old could only symbolize. Moreover, the old covenant was only temporary and transitory, but the new is permanent and final.

More to the point, under the old covenant, sacrifices had to be repeated daily, but the new covenant supplies a once-for-all efficacious sacrifice in the death of Christ (Heb. 10:4, 10–14). Old covenant sacrifices merely covered sins while pointing symbolically to the full atonement of the new covenant. That perfect, once-for-all atonement was supplied by Christ, who gathered up all the sins of all believers of all time and *took them away* in one act: offering His own body as "one sacrifice for sins for all time" (v. 12).

On top of that, as we have noted, old covenant worship was full of ceremonies and ritual. The new covenant has replaced all that with a new, more personal, enhanced ministry of the Holy Spirit. Whereas under the old covenant worshippers had to offer their sacrifices at the temple in Jerusalem, new covenant worshippers worship "in spirit and truth" anywhere (John 4:23).

So the point is that the incomplete and shadowy promises of the old covenant have, by God's gracious and sovereign purpose, given way to the fuller and more glorious promises of the new covenant (Heb. 8:6). The only way of salvation is, as always, by grace through faith. God has always forgiven and justified the repentant believer based on Jesus Christ's bearing the believer's sin on the cross. But the new covenant actually delivers the complete, once-for-all sacrifice that was only foreshadowed through the animal sacrifices of the old.

Take a look at Hebrews 9:11–14, which clearly spells out this great contrast between the old covenant and the new:

> But when Christ appeared as a high priest of the good things to come, He entered through the greater and more perfect tabernacle, not made with hands, that is to say, not of this creation; and not through the blood of goats and calves, but through His own blood, He entered the holy place once for all, having obtained eternal redemption. For if the blood of goats and bulls and the ashes of a heifer sprinkling those who have been defiled sanctify for the cleansing of the flesh, how much more will the blood of Christ, who through the eternal Spirit offered Himself without blemish to God, cleanse your conscience from dead works to serve the living God?

This passage makes the crucial point that all we need now is the new covenant. Whereas the high priest under the old covenant had to enter the Holy Place regularly throughout the year and the Holy of Holies once every year to offer sacrifice for sin, Christ had to offer Himself just once as the perfect sacrifice to forgive sins. Now that the substance is here, there is no point to return to the shadows. *We don't need a ritual system to maintain a right relationship with God.* Sadly, ritualism, so common in religions like Roman Catholicism, Eastern

Orthodoxy, and some high-church Protestant settings, only hinders the work of God's Spirit in enabling people to enjoy the benefits of the new covenant. The new covenant was not intended to be a system weighed down with ritualism. That's one of the very things that sets it apart from the old covenant.

Hebrews 8:7–8 states quite plainly that the old covenant had faults and deficiencies. The animal sacrifices and other ceremonial requirements of the law were not "faults" in the sense that they were evil elements, for God Himself ordained them. But they were inherently inadequate because they were merely symbolic, temporary, and never designed to be efficacious. That is why there had to be a new covenant. The remainder of Hebrews 8, which is mostly a quote of Jeremiah 31:31–34, gives us seven characteristics of the new covenant, showing how it is a better covenant.

It Is from God (Heb. 8:8)

The point the writer of Hebrews made, when he quoted from Jeremiah 31:31, is that the new covenant was God's sovereign plan from the beginning. He never planned to make the old covenant permanent. The new covenant is therefore not a change in the divine plan but a culmination of the plan He had from before the foundation of the world.

It Is Unique (Heb. 8:9)

God Himself stated that the new covenant is "not like the covenant which I made with their fathers on the day when I took them by the hand to lead them out of the land of Egypt." As we have seen, the new covenant is different because it replaces all the ceremony and symbolism with that which is efficacious and authentic. It replaces the ritualistic and external with realities that are spiritual and internal.

It is important to stress that the differences between the covenants are *qualitative* differences—not like the contrast between bad and good, but better and best. Francis Turretin wrote, "Moses is not opposed to Christ, but subordinated."[1] Jesus told the Pharisees, "If you believed Moses, you would believe Me, for he wrote about Me" (John 5:46). So the old covenant is not *antithetical* to the new, as some would teach; rather, the new is the definitive refinement and fulfillment of all God's gracious promises in the old.

It Is with Israel (Heb. 8:8–10)

God has always made His covenants only with Israel, which is why Jesus said in John 4:22, "Salvation is from the Jews." However, God's agreements with the Jews have never excluded the Gentiles from salvation (see Ex. 12:48; Lev. 19:33–34; Gal. 3:28–29). In fact, Israel was supposed to represent God to the rest of the world through the covenants.

It Is Not Legalistic (Heb. 8:9)

Verse 9 says the Jews "did not continue in My covenant." This underscores the impossibility of perfectly keeping legalistic and ritual requirements, which were a hallmark of all worship under the old covenant. The kind of legalistic ritualism that makes repeated sacrifices and ceremonial washings essential has no part in the new covenant, because Jesus' new covenant redemption is a once-for-all act that keeps us cleansed from sin (Heb. 7:25; 9:24–26).

It Is Internal (Heb. 8:10)

The new covenant is not based on external objects, such as stone tablets or parchment. Instead, it is characterized by a Spirit-generated heart attitude, which the prophet Ezekiel foresaw when he wrote, "I will put My Spirit within you" (Ezek. 36:27; see also Jer. 32:40). Also, under the new covenant, God's eternal moral law is inscribed upon the very hearts of the faithful (Jer. 31:33). (Later in this chapter we'll have more to say on the issue of the moral law.)

It Is Personal (Heb. 8:11)

If the new covenant is internal, it logically follows that it would be personal. By that I mean it has a personal, individual application, wrought by the Holy Spirit. This personal ministry of the Holy Spirit is one of the glorious advantages believers have under the new covenant, as Jesus promised in John 14:16: "I will ask the Father, and He will give you another Helper, that He may be with you forever."

It Provides Complete Forgiveness (Heb. 8:12)

As we have already alluded to, complete and final forgiveness of sins is the capstone of the new covenant. Under the old covenant, the sacrificial system could provide a symbolic covering for sins, but the basis for true forgiveness in Christ was merely anticipated in mystery (Isa. 53:10–12). But with the new covenant now here, we can enjoy in the full light of the glorious revelation of Christ, the total forgiveness He brings (Col. 2:13–14).

Isaac Watts, the great eighteenth-century English hymn writer and preacher, knew well that the new covenant is the better covenant. The first two stanzas of one of his lesser-known hymns testify to that:

Not all the blood of beasts on Jewish altars slain,
Could give the guilty conscience peace, or wash away the stain:
But Christ, the heav'nly Lamb takes all our sins away,
A sacrifice of nobler name and richer blood than they.

What about the Moral Law?

A very important foundational element of the old covenant that is still discussed today is the place of the law, and especially the Ten Commandments. These commandments are often associated with the old covenant in the minds of most Christians. Some even go so far as to suggest that under the new covenant, the moral law and the Ten Commandments no longer apply. They often cite Paul's words in Romans 6:14 as support for their position: "You are not under law but under grace."

In context, Paul was denying that the law is a means of justification (Rom. 3:20). He often used the expression "under law" to describe those who were seeking justification through means of the law (compare Gal. 4:21 with 5:4). So when he stated that we are "not under law" in Romans 6, he was underscoring the same point he made repeatedly, from beginning to end in Romans: True believers are not seeking to earn justification through obedience to the law. It is *that* sort of bondage to the law we are free from. We are free from the law's condemnation. We are free from the obligation to earn our own justifying righteousness.

We are *not* free from the moral obligations of the law, however. "What then? Shall we sin because we are not under law but under grace? May it never be!" (Rom. 6:15). The prohibitions against lying, stealing, bearing false witness, disobeying our parents, and so on—the moral requirements of the law—have not been abrogated.

How is it that the ceremonies and sacrifices required by the law are no longer in effect, but the law's moral requirements still are? To answer this question, it is important to know something about the various aspects of the law. The moral law is one of three components of the law, the others being the civil and ceremonial aspects.

Civil and Ceremonial Law

The civil aspect of the law was given by God to Israel to set those people apart as a unique nation. He needed to give the Israelites special instructions so that they could order their nation's social and economic life. These instructions and ordinances not only provided orderliness to the Israelite culture, but they also set boundaries that were intended to isolate God's people from the pagan cultures around them (see Ex. 21—23 and Deut. 12—28).

The ceremonial element of the law was given by God to the Israelites to govern proper worship. The ceremonial laws were those commandments that outlined all the types and symbols associated with the Levitical priesthood. As we have seen, these ceremonies only illustrated greater realities in the redemptive plan of God. For example, the animal sacrifices and the various washings were only symbolic of the atoning work of Christ and the sanctifying work of the Holy Spirit. Throughout the sequence of ceremonies the people were reminded of God's holiness, their own sinfulness, and their desperate need for salvation (see Ex. 25—29; 35—40, and the book of Lev.). So the ceremonial aspects of the law only illustrated God's redemptive purpose for His people. They were never really efficacious (Heb. 10:4), and thus they were never meant to be anything more than temporary laws.

Both the civil and the ceremonial aspects of old covenant law have therefore served their purposes and have been set aside. We might compare what has happened to the civil and ceremonial laws with what occurred during the energy shortages of the early and late 1970s. Some of us remember that in certain parts of the United States gasoline was in such short supply that systems of rationing were imposed. The odd/even method was most commonly used—people with even-numbered license plates were allowed to fuel their cars on even-numbered days, and people with odd-numbered license plates were allowed to come to the gas station on odd-numbered days. Happily, as fuel became more available after a few months, long-term rationing was not needed. Certainly no one today would want to return to any form of rationing when gas is now plentiful in comparison. Neither should Christians return to unnecessary civil and ceremonial components of God's law.

The apostle Paul clearly spelled out the abolishment of the civil and ceremonial laws under the new covenant. First, concerning the civil, he said,

> Therefore remember that formerly you, the Gentiles in the flesh, who are called "Uncircumcision" by the so-called "Circumcision," which is performed in the flesh by human hands—remember that you were at that time separate from Christ, excluded from the commonwealth of Israel, and strangers to the

> covenants of promise, having no hope and without God in the world. But now in Christ Jesus you who formerly were far off have been brought near by the blood of Christ. For He Himself is our peace, who made both groups into one and broke down the barrier of the dividing wall, by abolishing in His flesh the enmity, which is the Law of commandments contained in ordinances, so that in Himself He might make the two into one new man, thus establishing peace, and might reconcile them both in one body to God through the cross, by it having put to death the enmity. (Eph. 2:11–16)

Paul said more regarding the Gentiles' position within the body of Christ, and in so doing he pronounced the ceremonial law void:

> When you were dead in your transgressions and the uncircumcision of your flesh, He made you alive together with Him, having forgiven us all our transgressions, having canceled out the certificate of debt consisting of decrees against us, which was hostile to us; and He has taken it out of the way, having nailed it to the cross.... Therefore no one is to act as your judge in regard to food or drink or in respect to a festival or a new moon or a Sabbath day—things which are a mere shadow of what is to come; but the substance belongs to Christ. Let no one keep defrauding you of your prize by delighting

> in self-abasement and the worship of the angels, taking his stand on visions he has seen, inflated without cause by his fleshly mind, and not holding fast to the head, from whom the entire body, being supplied and held together by the joints and ligaments, grows with a growth which is from God. (Col. 2:13–14, 16–19)

Moral Law

Finally, there is the moral law. This is summarized well in the Ten Commandments, which in turn are summed up in the Two Great Commandments:

> "You shall love the Lord your God with all your heart, and with all your soul, and with all your mind" [Deut. 6:5]. This is the great and foremost commandment. The second is like it, "You shall love your neighbor as yourself" [Lev. 19:18]. On these two commandments depend the whole Law and the Prophets. (Matt. 22:37–40)

The *moral* law has to do with a person's ethical, moral, virtuous heart attitude, and with a person's behavior toward other people and toward God. The moral law is eternal. It reflects the very nature of God, was binding even before it was inscribed in stone on Mount Sinai, and remains in effect under the new covenant. Clearly the moral law was binding before Sinai, even upon the previous inhabitants of the Promised Land. In fact, the very reason God expelled them and gave the land to Israel was that they had violated His moral law (Lev. 18:24–28). The moral law is therefore the centerpiece of God's commandments to Moses and will never be abrogated. Therefore we need to consider its Spirit-guided purpose.

The moral law was given for three basic reasons. First, it was revealed to show us God's essence. Throughout the moral law the supreme representation of who He is, His holiness, is most clearly set forth. Moses and the children of Israel knew this truth even before the law was formally given in Exodus 20: "Who is like You among the gods, O LORD? Who is like You, majestic in holiness, awesome in praises, working wonders?" (Ex. 15:11).

Second, the moral law reveals God's will for humanity's behavior, which is what the Ten Commandments are concerned with. They teach us how we are to behave toward God (Ex. 20:3–11), and then they tell us how we are to behave morally and ethically toward other people (vv. 12–17).

Finally, the moral law shows us that we are sinners. As we realize God's holiness and becomes aware of His standards, the logical conclusion is that we will see how far short we fall from God's level (see Gal. 3:19–22). This is the impetus to repentance and calling on the mercy of God for gracious forgiveness. Old Testament conversions occurred when the penitent beat on his chest, as it were, with guilt over his sin and frustration at the inability to do anything about it. Pleading for God's grace was his only hope.

So what is the proper, scriptural answer to our earlier question about the place of the moral law in the life of the new covenant believer? D. Martyn Lloyd-Jones answered the question and provided an excellent summary for our brief consideration of the moral law:

> The position with regard to this [the moral law] is different, because here God is laying down something which is permanent and perpetual, the relationship which must always subsist between Himself and man. It is all to be found, of course, in what our Lord calls the first and greatest commandment. "Thou shalt love the Lord thy God with all thy heart, and with all thy soul, and with all thy strength, and with all thy mind." That is permanent. That is not for the theocratic nation only; it is for the whole of mankind. The second commandment, He says, "is like unto it, Thou shalt love thy neighbour as thyself." That again was not only for the theocratic nation of Israel; that was not merely the old ceremonial law. It is a permanent condition and part of our perpetual relationship to God. Thus the moral law, as interpreted by the New Testament, stands now as much as it has ever done, and will do so until the end of time and until we are perfected. In I John iii the apostle is very careful to remind his readers that sin in Christian people is still "a transgression of the law." "We still see our relationship to the law," says John in effect, "for sin is a transgression of the law." The law is still there, and when I sin I am breaking that law, though I am

> a Christian and though I have never been a Jew, and am a Gentile. So the moral law still applies to us.[2]

Jesus gave the moral law new commentary (Matt. 5—7) and a new summary (e.g., Mark 12:28–34), but He did not abolish it or say that because He was the mediator of a better covenant the moral law no longer mattered (see especially Matt. 5:17–18). In our eagerness to see the glories of the new covenant and the Holy Spirit's fullness in it, we must take care not to discard God's unchanging standards of righteous conduct.

Contrasting Covenants

With the inclusion of the moral law the new covenant is strengthened as the better covenant. In that contrasting role to the old covenant, the new opened the way for a more complete manifestation of the Holy Spirit. That spiritual contrast between the two covenants had already been foreseen in the old: "'But this is the covenant which I will make with the house of Israel after those days,' declares the LORD, 'I will put My law within them and on their heart I will write it; and I will be their God, and they shall be My people'" (Jer. 31:33). Joel 2:28–32 also strongly implies that the new covenant era would be a time of greater activity by the Holy Spirit (this idea was verified by the apostle Peter in Acts 2:16–21).

In 2 Corinthians 3 the apostle Paul alluded to the Spirit-filled quality of the new covenant when he described the believers he knew in Corinth: "You are our letter, written in our hearts, known and read by all men; being manifested that you are a letter of Christ, cared for by us, written not with ink but with the Spirit of the living God, not on tablets of stone but on tablets of human hearts" (2 Cor. 3:2–3). Such implementation of the new covenant in the lives of believers was closely related to the work of the Spirit. This message, written on human hearts, contained the laws of the new covenant that were in reality not external laws, but virtues blossoming into fruit under the gracious influence of the Spirit.

Further on in 2 Corinthians 3, as if to underscore the contrast between the covenants, Paul demonstrated the greater glory of the new covenant. The apostle returned to the narrative in Exodus 34 in which Moses was coming back down from Mount Sinai after receiving a new set of tablets from God. The stone tablets contained the Ten Commandments and replaced the tablets destroyed by an angry Moses over the golden calf incident. While he was on the mountain, Moses communed with God and glimpsed some of His glory.

During the time of Moses' ministry, God manifested His spiritual presence by reducing all His attributes to visible light. God appeared a number of times in the book of Exodus as the *shekinah* glory, most notably as the cloud by day and the pillar of fire by night that led the people of Israel. The *shekinah* also filled the tabernacle when it was completed (Ex. 40:34–38).

Having been in God's presence, Moses' face shone brightly, almost like an incandescent lightbulb, when he came down from the mountain. His face was so bright that Aaron and the people were frightened and could not bear to look directly at him. Moses solved those difficulties by placing a veil over his face whenever he was not meeting with God or speaking God's words directly to the people.

Paul explained his point, beginning in 2 Corinthians 3:7. The old covenant law came with glory, but a glory that was limited. This glory was reflected in Moses' face and was apparent to everyone who saw him. Because the law was from God, it also reflected His character and His will. (The apostle wanted to be sure that his readers knew that he was not against the law, as his critics had claimed he was.) Nevertheless, as we will note in the following chapter, the glory of the law, like the glow on Moses' face, was a fading glory.

In 2 Corinthians 3:9, Paul summarized his assertion about the glory of the law: "For if the ministry of condemnation has glory, much more does the ministry of righteousness abound in glory." This verse again reminds us of the law's limited role and capabilities. It could only show sinners their condition and point them to the need for salvation—by itself the law could not save (see Gal. 3:23–25).

Nevertheless, the law had a glory of its own. It is holy, just, and good (Rom. 7:12). But the glory of divine grace revealed in the new covenant is far superior.

Paul's conclusion regarding the contrast between the covenants is obvious: "For if that which fades away was with glory, much more that which remains is in glory" (2 Cor. 3:11). If the old covenant ("the ministry of condemnation"), temporary though it was, had such vivid glory, the new covenant ("the ministry of righteousness") certainly has as much glory and more. The Holy Spirit made it clear to Paul that the new covenant is indeed the better covenant. And the Holy Spirit clearly encourages us to rejoice in the reality of the better covenant as well.

Our Silent Shepherd, the Holy Spirit, wants to lead us into the full glories and superiorities of the new covenant, for in reality the new covenant is "the ministry of the Spirit" (2 Cor. 3:8).

4

THE SPIRIT OF TRANSFORMATION AND HOPE

During my years of travel and ministry I have received and collected some fascinating memorabilia. One of my most precious pieces is a small, obscure-looking pencil etching. Every time I view this little picture, my heart is moved and I feel my eyes moisten.

The drawing portrays three figures. One is a fierce-looking Moses holding the tablets of stone over his head. He is poised to bring them down onto the head of a second figure, who is a bedraggled, fragile person with a wan expression of despair. The third figure is Jesus Christ, who is embracing the frail soul, with His arms completely around the person's chest and His shoulders shielding the person's head.

Beyond the basic interpretation of the drawing, that Christ can protect the helpless individual from being clobbered by the tablets of the law, every time I look at that little picture, I marvel at the profound doctrinal truth it depicts. The artist masterfully showed the difference between the law and the gospel of grace. The law, represented by Moses and the tablets, presents us with a hopeless outlook and seeks to smash us. It threatens, but it cannot save. The gospel, represented by Christ, gives us new life and protects us from all the condemning blows of the law. The law cannot save us; it simply shows us our sinful, helpless condition. The gospel does provide a secure salvation for all who trust in Christ.

As the apostle John wrote, "The Law was given through Moses; grace and truth were realized through Jesus Christ" (John 1:17). The old covenant delivered the law in all its fullness and glory. The law itself is not evil; its function is to reveal the sinfulness of sin and the absolute righteousness of God (Rom. 7:7). But the law condemns those who violate it, and it shows no mercy (see Heb. 10:28; James 2:10).

The new covenant does for grace what the Mosaic covenant did for law. It reveals grace in all its fullness and glory. It unveils the glorious truth of the gospel and the way of redemption through Christ—something the old covenant only revealed in types and figures.

As we saw in chapter 3, the new covenant has a better foundation and better promises. It possesses a brilliant, lasting glory that will not fade away like the glory of the old covenant (see Ex. 34:29–35; 2 Cor. 3:7–11). But there are other qualities that make the new covenant superior. Insight into those distinctives will give us greater motivation than ever to obey the Holy Spirit in living an abundant Christian life.

A Covenant of Life

The new covenant is superior first of all because its focus is on grace and truth, forgiveness and life. The apostle Paul told the Corinthian church, "[God] also made us adequate as servants of a new covenant, not of the letter but of the Spirit; for the letter kills, but the Spirit gives life" (2 Cor. 3:6). Thus he uniquely linked the Holy Spirit to the new covenant.

How the Letter Kills

Paul used the term *letter* more than as a mere synonym for the law. Instead, he used it to mean a distortion of the true intention of the law, which was to lead a person to recognize his or her sinfulness, hopelessness, and helplessness before a holy God, and to repent, seeking mercy. "The letter" in Paul's terminology refers to the external requirements of the law, wrongly thought to be a means of justification. The law condemned sinners and therefore should have driven sinners to despair of achieving God's favor by means of any system of works. Once the sinner realized his or her hopelessness, God's word to him or her, in the prophet Isaiah's words, was that the guilty one "seek the Lord while He may be found; call upon Him while He is near. Let the wicked forsake his way and the unrighteous man his thoughts; and let him return to the Lord, and He will have compassion on him, and to our God, for He will abundantly pardon" (Isa. 55:6–7). That was a clear promise of salvation and forgiveness by grace.

Instead of following this path, however, most of the Jews continued seeking to establish their own righteousness through attempting to obey the letter of the law. "Not knowing about God's righteousness and seeking to establish their own, they did not subject themselves to the righteousness of God" (Rom. 10:3). They were "seeking to be justified by law" (Gal. 5:4). "The letter" in Pauline usage, is an expression that describes this form of legalism, where the law is seen as an instrument of justification.

The apostle Paul, in his years as a Pharisee, learned from bitter firsthand experience that the letter could only kill.

Living Death

The letter created a living death for Paul: "I was once alive apart from the Law; but when the commandment came, sin became alive and I died; and this commandment, which was to result in life, proved to result in death for me; for sin, taking opportunity through the commandment, deceived me and through it killed me" (Rom. 7:9–11). Paul thought he was righteous until he really confronted the law of God. Then it killed any confidence, joy, or peace of mind he may have had and replaced them with frustration, guilt, sorrow, and despair. That was in effect a living death for Paul.

Spiritual Death

The letter produced death for Paul spiritually as well. He stated this truth very plainly in Galatians 3:10: "For as many as are of the works of the Law are under a curse; for it is written, 'Cursed is everyone who does not abide by all things written in the book of the Law, to perform them.'" The curse he referred to involves much more than the living death of Romans 7, and it certainly connotes much more than some superstitious concept of bad luck. Paul was talking about damnation, being spiritually lost, or being separated from God forever.

The only way to escape this curse is to let the law do its rightful work in our hearts, as the tax collector experienced in Jesus' parable: "But the tax collector [in contrast to the Pharisee], standing some distance away, was even unwilling to lift up his eyes to heaven, but was beating his breast, saying, 'God be merciful to me, the sinner!'" (Luke 18:13). The law can point out our sinful condition, and by repentance and faith, we can move from a recognition of our sin to the covenant of life.

Ceremonialism

Paul also knew the letter killed in a most devastating way through ceremonialism. Ceremonialism can have such harmful spiritual results because it is so subtly deceptive. It often becomes an end in itself by convincing people that all they need is faithfulness to the elements of the ceremony—consistent performance of rituals that will make them right with God. Paul said that this deception is what happened to the Jews: "Israel, pursuing a law of righteousness, did not arrive at that law. Why? Because they did not pursue it by faith, but as though it were by works" (Rom. 9:31–32).

The deception of ceremonialism is the most deadly of the ways the letter of the law can kill. It cuts short the law's various opportunities to point sinners toward salvation. Ceremonialism gives people a comfortable but false sense of security in a ritual system of worship. Reliance on religious ceremony tends to place symbols, liturgies, and formats between a person's heart and the message of the gospel.

How the Spirit Gives Life

If the centerpiece of the old covenant was the law, the centerpiece of the new covenant is Christ and the full, free forgiveness He offers sinners who turn to Him. This eternal life does not come by external means. The Holy Spirit, whose work is internal, grants it:

> Moreover, I will give you a new heart and put a new spirit within you; and I will remove the heart of stone from your flesh and give you a heart of flesh. I will put My Spirit within you and cause you to walk in My statutes, and you will be careful to observe my ordinances. (Ezek. 36:26–27)

Whereas the law alone could only kill, the Spirit gives life.

A Permanent Covenant

A permanent agreement is almost always preferable to something temporary. For instance, the Sears retail chain is famous for promising lifelong satisfaction for its merchandise, especially its line of tools, hardware, and automotive parts. Whenever one of these items breaks or wears out from normal use, Sears promises to provide the customer a new one at no charge. This kind of guarantee is certainly better than one that is short-term and maybe not well-defined. In those cases a product often seems to fail or wear out just after the one- or two-year warranty period has expired. The owner is then left with no other option but to buy a replacement for the item or do without one.

The average person derives much more important peace of mind in knowing that certain other legal, financial, or political agreements are long-term and secure. A guaranteed rate of return for the life of an investment is often a good arrangement. A permanent peace treaty between nations is certainly preferable to war every few years or an uneasy cease-fire that leaves tensions and differences unresolved for decades.

The new covenant, with its permanent character, gives believers in Christ far more security than any lifetime agreement in this world ever could. The new covenant's permanency is a second reason for its superiority over the old. The writer to the Hebrews, in speaking about Jesus as the better priest or mediator of the new covenant, said this:

> For it is attested of Him, "You are a priest forever according to the order of Melchizedek." For, on the one hand, there is a setting aside of a former commandment because of its weakness and uselessness (for the Law made nothing perfect), and on the other hand there is a bringing in of a better hope, through which we draw near to God.... The former priests, on the one hand, existed in greater numbers because they were prevented by death from continuing, but Jesus, on the other hand, because He continues forever, holds His priesthood permanently. (Heb. 7:17–19, 23–24)

If Jesus is the priest of a better covenant—a fact we established in chapter 3—and His priesthood is permanent, then we must conclude that the new covenant is also permanent. With similar logic, Hebrews 7 shows us that the "former priests" were temporary and inferior to Christ; therefore, the old covenant was also temporary and inferior to the permanent new covenant.

The old covenant was never meant to be the last word on humanity's plight and how sinners could become right with God.

As we have seen repeatedly, the law cannot save but merely points to something greater—the new covenant in Christ. Christ alone offers salvation. In this sense the new covenant is the final word, the permanent word on salvation by grace through faith. It represents the permanent unveiling of what the old covenant only hinted at.

We can rejoice that the new covenant is permanent and will never be replaced. If we have trusted Him, we are complete in Jesus Christ, the Good Shepherd, who has once and forever accomplished the redemption of His people (1 Peter 3:18). We are also complete in the Holy Spirit, the Silent Shepherd, who transforms us (John 3:5) and leads us into all truth (16:13). Our completeness in Christ and the Spirit demonstrates that all the spiritual reality we'll ever need is in the new covenant. We don't need to look ahead for some additional revelation or extra experience; neither should we look backward and pattern our worship after obsolete ceremonies and rituals from the old covenant era (see Gal. 3:3).

A Clear Covenant

The new covenant is also superior because of its clarity, which stands in striking contrast to the veiled quality of the old. Concealment was inherent in the fading glory of the old covenant. Paul explained this concealment by means of an analogy to Moses in Exodus 34 (2 Cor. 3:13–16).

Remember that when Moses came down from Mount Sinai, his face brought the reflection of God's glory down from the mountain. That old covenant glory, even though fading, was still too blinding and deadly for the Israelites to view. Therefore, Moses had to adopt the following strategy: "Whenever Moses went in before the LORD to speak with Him, he would take off the veil until he came out; and whenever he came out and spoke to the sons of Israel what he had been commanded, the sons of Israel would see the face of Moses, that the skin of Moses' face shone. So Moses would replace the veil over his face until he went in to speak with Him" (Ex. 34:34–35). (The reflection on Moses' face faded away between the times he spoke to God.)

Moses' veiled face symbolized the old covenant's concealment and its essentially shadowy character. But there is nothing veiled or concealed about the new covenant gospel. Paul knew that to be true when he wrote: "By revelation there was made known to me the mystery, as I wrote before in brief. By referring to this, when you read you can understand my insight into the mystery of Christ, which in other generations was not made known to the sons of men, as it has now been revealed to His holy apostles and prophets in the Spirit" (Eph. 3:3–5). What the old covenant left hidden concerning the gospel and God's kingdom, the new covenant makes very clear. That clarity is sharply focused through the Spirit-guided lens of New Testament Scripture.

There is more to the old covenant's obscurity than shrouded concealment and murky symbols and types. The Jews' unbelief was the additional factor that made the old covenant even less clear: "Their minds were made dull, for to this day the same veil remains when the old covenant is read. It has not been removed, because only in Christ is it taken away" (2 Cor. 3:14 NIV; see also Heb. 3:8, 15; 4:7). This unbelief led most Jews to a complete misunderstanding of the old covenant's true purpose and no comprehension of the new covenant's meaning. Even some of the disciples had difficulty comprehending the old covenant's purpose and its transition to the new. The disciples who were on the road to Emmaus the day of Jesus' resurrection illustrated this point well. They did not even recognize Jesus when He joined them along the road; neither was the meaning of His death clear:

> [Jesus] said to them, "O foolish men and slow of heart to believe in all that the prophets have spoken! Was it not necessary for the Christ to suffer these things and to enter into His glory?" Then beginning with Moses and with all the prophets, He explained to them the things concerning Himself in all the Scriptures. (Luke 24:25–27; read 24:13–32 for the complete context.)

In sharp contrast to the Israelites or the Emmaus disciples, we should be absolutely sure of the new covenant's clarity and superiority—just as Paul was: "Therefore having such a hope, we use great boldness in our speech, and are not like Moses, who used to put a veil over his face so that the sons of Israel would not look intently at the end of what was fading away" (2 Cor. 3:12–13).

A Christ-Centered Covenant

More than anything else, the life and ministry of our Lord Jesus Christ allows us to see the glories of the new covenant. His work of redemption is the centerpiece of the covenant, defining it and showing its superiority over the old. When anyone is drawn by faith to Jesus Christ, the veil is lifted and everything makes sense concerning the new covenant. Through the regenerating and sanctifying work of the Holy Spirit, God brings light out of darkness and shadows. The apostle Paul expressed it this way: "For God, who said, 'Light shall shine out of darkness,' is the One who has shone in our hearts to give the Light of the knowledge of the glory of God in the face of Christ" (2 Cor. 4:6).

The wonderful advantage of the new covenant is that we can see, with the eyes of faith, the unobscured glory of God by looking at the face of Jesus. We no longer have to deal with the inferior components and ritual requirements of the old covenant to have salvation or a clear view of God's will for us. We don't have to be perplexed by passages in the prophetic books anymore (see Acts 8:30–35). Instead, all things now become clear in Christ.

When Paul used the expression "glory of God," in 2 Corinthians 4:6, he was referring to God's manifest attributes, and they were all embodied in Christ (see also v. 4; John 1:14). The presence of God's glory in Christ was most dramatically demonstrated for Peter, James, and John at the transfiguration (Luke 9:28–36). Peter reiterated the significance of that event years later in his second letter:

> We were eyewitnesses of His majesty. For when He received honor and glory from God the Father, such an utterance as this was made to Him by the Majestic Glory, "This is My beloved Son with whom I am well-pleased"—and we ourselves heard this utterance made from heaven when we

> were with Him on the holy mountain. (2 Peter 1:16–18)

The Christ-centered new covenant makes it possible, by God's grace and the Holy Spirit's power, for us to know the same glorious truth.

A Covenant of Hope

A covenant that is Christ-centered is bound to be one that brings hope. The new covenant fully unveils the hope of the believer. With the unveiling of this glorious hope came the passing away of the endless sacrifices of the old covenant and the burdensome ceremonialism.

Hope is the strong and confident belief that the promises of God will be fulfilled. Some of these have already come to pass, such as the forgiveness of sins (Matt. 1:21; John 1:29), the destroying of sin's grip (Rom. 5:6–11; 6:10–11), the abundant life (John 10:10), and eternal life (John 5:24). But some of the new covenant's promises have not yet been fully realized. That will happen in heaven. The apostle Paul knew that such hope is inherent in the new covenant. In Romans 8:18–25 he looked ahead with anticipation to "the freedom of the glory of the children of God" (v. 21). After beginning this passage by contrasting present suffering with the far better glory that awaits all believers, Paul concluded with a reminder that our new covenant hope is real:

> We ourselves, having the first fruits of the Spirit, even we ourselves groan within ourselves, waiting eagerly for our adoption as sons, the redemption

> of our body. For in hope we have been saved, but hope that is seen is not hope; for who hopes for what he already sees? But if we hope for what we do not see, with perseverance we wait eagerly for it. (Rom. 8:23–25)

The apostle Peter fully agreed with Paul that new covenant believers have much to hope in. In the opening of his first letter, Peter assured all Christians: "Blessed be the God and Father of our Lord Jesus Christ, who according to His great mercy has caused us to be born again to a living hope through the resurrection of Jesus Christ from the dead" (1 Peter 1:3). As if to underscore the importance of this great truth, Peter repeated it twice more in his first chapter, once as an exhortation (v. 13) and once as a reminder (v. 21).

Hope is a very important and encouraging theme that reappears many places in the New Testament. During His earthly ministry, Jesus certainly offered hope to people. Paul talked of hope in most of his letters. The book of Hebrews, the best and most complete New Testament treatment of the nature and superiority of the new covenant, provides this excellent summary regarding our hope: "This hope we have as an anchor of the soul, a hope both sure and steadfast and one which enters within the veil, where Jesus has entered as a forerunner for us" (Heb. 6:19–20).

A Transforming Covenant

The old covenant revealed what we *ought* to be—what God demands of us. The new covenant reveals what we *will* be in Christ. The apostle

John wrote, "Beloved, now we are children of God, and it has not appeared as yet what we will be. We know that when He appears, *we will be like Him*, because we will see Him just as He is" (1 John 3:2). This is the pinnacle of the new covenant's glory, the reason for our hope, and the goal of the Holy Spirit's work in us: We are being fashioned into the image of Christ.

The Holy Spirit has the central role in the process of our sanctification. He is transforming us from the inside out. Unlike Moses, whose glory was a fading, external reflection, the glory that is to be revealed in us is emerging from the inside out and growing brighter with each passing day. We "are being transformed into the same image from glory to glory, just as from the Lord, the Spirit" (2 Cor. 3:18).

One of the best-known stories by the nineteenth-century Danish writer Hans Christian Andersen is the fable "The Ugly Duckling." It is the story of a bird that was larger, more awkward, and less attractive than the other ducklings. They made fun of his clumsiness and bizarre appearance. Crushed and forlorn, the ugly duckling sought refuge at a home where the people had a cat and a chicken as pets. But those pets also spurned him because he couldn't purr or lay eggs.

"You don't understand me," the ugly duckling complained, but the other animals only ridiculed him all the more.

One day while the ugly duckling was paddling around the pond, trying his best to be just like the other ducks, he caught sight of some beautiful and graceful swans. Immediately he thought the swans were the best-looking birds he had ever seen. As the ugly duckling watched the graceful movements of the swans, a strange feeling came over him. He couldn't take his eyes off the swans, and he couldn't shake the new sense of destiny that for some reason overwhelmed him. Soon the swans flew off. As the ugly duckling stretched his neck and tried to follow the swans' flight path, he felt more love for them than for anything he had ever loved before.

During the cold winter months the ugly duckling thought about the lovely birds he had seen on the pond. He had no idea what they were called or where they came from, but he very much hoped to see them again. The spring weather finally arrived and melted the ice covering the pond. The ugly duckling was able to swim again, and one day in the early spring he saw two more of the beautiful birds on the pond. They swam straight toward him, and fear gripped his heart. He was embarrassed to have such elegant creatures see what an unattractive, clumsy bird he was.

As the swans approached him, the ugly duckling bowed his head in humility and covered his face with his wings. Just then he was surprised to see, for the first time, his own reflection in the water. To his amazement, he looked exactly like the beautiful birds. He was no longer an ugly duckling. In fact, he was not a duck at all—he was a swan. As he removed his wings from his face and lifted his head, his neck remained slightly bowed in gratitude and humility.

The fable of the ugly duckling illustrates the final superiority of the new covenant—it is transforming. When we are new Christians and first look at Christ, our experiences are often similar to the ugly duckling's when he first saw the swans. We have an overwhelming sense of sinfulness and unworthiness and yet an irresistible attraction to Christ that transforms our hearts. We respond from our innermost beings because we know He represents all we were made to be. It is both humbling and exciting to realize that we are being transformed more and more into the image of Christ—and this is distinctly a new covenant process that is accomplished under the guidance of the Holy Spirit.

With divine insight, the apostle Paul superbly captured the essence of the transforming operation: "But we all, with unveiled face, beholding as in a mirror the glory of the Lord, are being transformed into the same image from glory to glory, just as from the Lord, the Spirit" (2 Cor. 3:18). This verse has always been particularly precious to me. In fact, several years ago I wrote a booklet based on it, titled *My Favorite Verse*. More than any other verse I know, this one emphasizes the glorious nature of what Christ does for believers. The verse summarizes very well the theme of our chapter, that the new covenant is far more glorious than and superior to the old covenant.

God's transformation process will begin once we are fully saved and see with clarity the face of Christ and realize that here is God's glory (2 Cor. 4:6). We may not see the glory of the Lord perfectly (after all, polished metal mirrors were used in Paul's time—and they hardly gave the sharp reflected view that modern mirrors do), but we see it so much more clearly now that the old covenant veil is gone. The Greek word translated "being transformed" is *metamorphoo*, from which we get our word *metamorphosis* ("a striking alteration in appearance, character, or circumstances"). The Holy Spirit's transforming work is a continual, progressive one in which we are changed from one level of Christlikeness to another.

Second Corinthians 3:18 refers to progressive sanctification for all new covenant believers. The change "from glory to glory" is such a wonderful contrast to the diminishing glory that Moses experienced. Therefore, it is hard to understand why anyone would want to look back to the fading, inferior glories of the old covenant when the blessings of the new are here. Christ and the Spirit have set us free from the bondage of the letter (2 Cor. 3:17; Gal. 5:1).

The sanctification of believers is the goal of the new covenant. For those who are truly looking by faith, under the guidance of the Holy Spirit, to the face of Christ, there is no way they will not reach that goal: "For those whom He foreknew, He also predestined to become conformed to the image of His Son, so that He would be the firstborn among many brethren; and these whom He predestined, He also called; and these whom He called, He also justified; and these whom He justified, He also glorified" (Rom. 8:29–30).

Knowing and appreciating the crucial differences between the old and new covenants is very important—and it's a giant step forward in any believer's understanding of the Holy Spirit's working in this age. But the path to sanctification is difficult without a solid grasp of the specifics of the Spirit's new covenant presence and work. We'll begin to look at these in our next chapter.

5

THE PROMISED SPIRIT: A COMPLETE ARRIVAL

The year 1995 marked the fiftieth anniversary of the end of World War II. Many pages of print and minutes of airtime recalled the events that brought the biggest war in history to a conclusion. One thing that stood out to me in many of those accounts was how Americans at the end of the war looked to the future optimistically. In 1945, the United States was unquestionably the strongest military and economic power in the world. Americans at that time were poised to return to peacetime lifestyles and claim their portion of the American dream—owning a home and car, having a well-paying and secure job, seeing their children obtain quality educations and good jobs, and enjoying a pleasant and prosperous retirement. The promises of international peace and domestic prosperity were quite realistic to most people.

However, hopes for a long period of world peace were quickly shattered by several regional conflicts (e.g., the 1948 Arab-Israeli war; the fall of China to the Communists in 1949). The sense of unease was only made worse by the early tensions of the Cold War (e.g., the Berlin airlift and the first Soviet atomic bomb, both in 1948–49). Even the end of the Cold War did not bring an end to international hostilities, as the Persian Gulf War and the civil war in Bosnia demonstrated soon afterward.

Most Americans were economically prosperous and secure during the first decades after World War II. But in the past forty years the American economy has become much more volatile. Its basic nature began changing sixty years ago from a manufacturing base to a service and information base. As this trend continued, it eliminated many high-paying, secure jobs. Taxes and the cost of living have increased, while income, adjusted for inflation, has stayed about the same for many Americans. Huge national debts and deficits have further discouraged many younger people concerning their economic futures.

The national and international outlooks might be more complicated and uncertain now than they were for those who remember end-of-the-war euphoria over sixty-five years ago. However, the world's promises have always been fleeting and unpredictable. In contrast, Scripture's promises remain reliable. Christians living under the new covenant can count on a pledge that is absolutely secure and more comforting than anything the world can offer.

Jesus' Promise of the Spirit

Jesus' promise to send the Holy Spirit, our Silent Shepherd, is one of the most important ones Scripture ever recorded.

Our Lord spelled it out first to His disciples:

> I will ask the Father, and He will give you another Helper, that He may be with you forever; that is the Spirit of truth, whom the world cannot receive, because it does not see Him or know Him, but you know Him because He abides with you and will be in you.
>
> I will not leave you as orphans; I will come to you. (John 14:16–18)

This guarantee was given in the early part of Jesus' Upper Room Discourse, the night before His crucifixion. Jesus' words of hope came at a crucial time for the disciples, who were confused and troubled at the prospect of His death and departure. The promise to send forth His Spirit is also part of the Lord's rich legacy to all believers right now.

Jesus' Pattern of Spirit-Led Ministry

From the earliest days of the Holy Spirit's ministry, it was evident that the He would have a major role in what Jesus would say and do. Jesus' baptism is a prime illustration: "After being baptized, Jesus came up immediately from the water; and behold, the heavens were opened, and he [John the Baptist] saw the Spirit of God descending as a dove and lighting on Him, and behold, a voice out of the heavens said, 'This is My beloved Son, in whom I am well-pleased'" (Matt. 3:16–17).

All that Christ did, He accomplished by the power and energy of the Spirit (see Acts 1:1–2). For example, Jesus' many miracles and the people's reaction to them demonstrated that His ministry was supernaturally empowered (read how the disciples reacted to His calming the storm in Matthew 8:23–27). His opposition (most notably the Pharisees), on the other hand, did not acknowledge the Spirit's role in His ministry. In fact, the Pharisees astoundingly came to the conclusion that Jesus was empowered by Satan. Their blasphemous accusation prompted Jesus to issue a strong public statement defending His actions and declaring the Spirit His real source of power (Matt. 12:22–37).

Our Lord summarized the seriousness of the Pharisees' ungodly attitude and their false conclusion that He was empowered by Satan:

> He who is not with Me is against Me; and he who does not gather with Me scatters.
>
> Therefore I say to you, any sin and blasphemy shall be forgiven people, but blasphemy against the Spirit shall not be forgiven. Whoever speaks a word against the Son of Man, it shall be forgiven him; but whoever speaks against the Holy Spirit, it shall not be forgiven him, either in this age or in the age to come. (Matt. 12:30–32)

Christ was most intent on making it clear that whatever mighty works people saw Him perform, they were also seeing evidence of the Spirit's working. Jesus was less concerned with criticism of Himself as the Son of Man than He was with blasphemy of the unseen person—the Holy Spirit—who energized His ministry.

Jesus is truly a model for us in His respect for the person and work of the Holy Spirit.

The Substance of Jesus' Promise

In His Upper Room Discourse, the Lord Jesus was very earnest regarding His promise to send the Holy Spirit. The substance of His pledge goes far beyond routine advice given only to the disciples—it has great implications for all new covenant believers.

Jesus' overall promise regarding the Spirit consists of four supernatural elements.

Supernatural Helper

First, He promised to send a *supernatural Helper* (John 14:16). Most immediately, this would fill the void left for the disciples when Jesus ended His earthbound ministry and ascended to heaven. "Helper" is the *New American Standard* translation of the Greek *parakletos*, "one called alongside to help." The word could also be rendered "advocate," which suggests a legal or courtroom meaning. *Advocate* implies the idea of either an attorney or a friend of the court. He could testify on our behalf or assist us with our case.

Christ, through the apostle John, was careful to use the right adjective in describing the Helper. The Lord chose the precise form of *another* because He wanted to communicate accurately the full definition of *Helper*. He used the Greek *allos*, which means "another that is identical." In other words, Jesus said that He will not be physically with us, but He is sending us precisely the same kind of Helper as He was. Except now the Holy Spirit resides within: "The Spirit of truth … abides with you and will be in you" (John 14:17).

Supernatural Life

Second, Jesus promised a *supernatural life*. Our lives will be different when we have the Holy Spirit. We know that is true simply by realizing what happens at the new birth (John 3:3–16; 2 Cor. 5:17; Eph. 2:4–5). With regeneration, Jesus assured us that our perspective will be different from the world's: "After a little while the world will no longer see Me, but you will see Me; because I live, you will live also" (John 14:19; see also 1 Cor. 2:12–14). When we are spiritually alive, we'll be sensitive to Christ's working in the world and begin to see things from God's viewpoint. The wonder of supernatural life is that Jesus also promised us His *own* spirit, not merely the Holy Spirit in some isolated fashion (John 14:18; see also Eph. 1:13; Col. 1:27).

Supernatural Teacher

Jesus also assured us that the Spirit would come as a *supernatural Teacher*: "The Helper, the Holy Spirit, whom the Father will send in My name, He will teach you all things, and bring to your remembrance all that I said to you" (John 14:26). This permanent teaching role is one of the most crucial aspects of the Spirit's ministry. It reminds us of our complete dependence on Christ and that we need His and the Holy Spirit's provision to nourish our spiritual lives (John 15:5).

We first need the Holy Spirit to give us an initial understanding of the truth (see John 6:63; 1 Cor. 2:10–15). But we also need His ongoing assistance if we hope to grow in our knowledge of that truth (John 16:13). Even the disciples, who had spent three years with Jesus, did not always understand everything right away. Several places in the gospel of John refer to the disciples' belated understanding of truth or their inability to receive it all at once (John 2:22; 12:16; 16:12). As we'll see in upcoming chapters, the Holy Spirit is available on a daily basis to meet our every need.

Supernatural Peace

The final element promised with the Holy Spirit's coming is a *supernatural peace*. This is what Jesus assured the disciples about in John 14:27: "Peace I leave with you; My peace I give to you; not as the world gives do I give to you. Do not let your heart be troubled, nor let it be fearful." This spiritual peace is far better than any peace of mind the world can offer through drugs, false psychology, New Age religion, or superficial political and diplomatic agreements. This peace is also different from the peace with God that Paul expounded in Romans 5:1–11 (see also Eph. 2:14–18; James 2:23), which is essential—it deals with our position before God—but does not always directly affect our life circumstances.

But Jesus did promise a peace that affects our daily circumstances. It aggressively and positively devours our troubles and turns them into joy. It keeps us from being victimized by events and gives us that inner tranquillity of soul that Paul spoke of in Philippians 4:7: "The peace of God, which surpasses all comprehension, will guard your hearts and your minds in Christ Jesus." This is a peace that transcends our understanding simply because it comes from God, not from the world and what happens to us.

The basis of this extraordinary peace is all three persons of the Trinity. In John 14:27, Jesus said, "My peace I give to you" (see also Acts 10:36; 2 Thess. 3:16; Heb. 7:2). First Thessalonians 5:23 tells of the Father's role: "Now may the God of peace Himself sanctify you entirely" (see also 1 Cor. 14:33; Phil. 4:9; Heb. 13:20). Finally, the Holy Spirit has the key role as a dispenser of peace: "The fruit of the Spirit is love, joy, peace, patience, kindness, goodness, faithfulness, gentleness, self-control; against such things there is no law" (Gal. 5:22–23).

Of course, loving obedience is crucial to our full enjoyment of the supernatural promises. Jesus reminded the disciples of this when He promised to send another Helper: "He who has My commandments and keeps them is the one who loves Me; and he who loves Me will be loved by My Father, and I will love him and will disclose Myself to him" (John 14:21; see also v. 23). Our Lord went on to reveal the key to obedience in this well-known reference to the vine and the branches: "I am the vine, you are the branches; he who abides in Me and I in him, he bears much fruit, for apart from Me you can do nothing" (John 15:5; see also 1 John 5:3–7). The key is intimacy with Christ.

The Need for Jesus' Promise

Jesus' promise of the Holy Spirit was given purposefully, within the larger scope of God's sovereign plan. The apostle Peter attested to this in his Pentecost sermon:

> Jesus the Nazarene, a man attested to you by God with miracles and wonders and signs which God performed through Him in your midst, just as you yourselves know—this Man, delivered over by the predetermined plan and foreknowledge of God, you nailed to a cross by the hands of godless

> men and put Him to death. But God raised Him up again, putting an end to the agony of death, since it was impossible for Him to be held in its power.... Therefore having been exalted to the right hand of God, and having received from the Father the promise of the Holy Spirit, He has poured forth this which you both see and hear. (Acts 2:22–24, 33)

Because God has sovereignly given us the Holy Spirit, we should be convinced of our need for His shepherding role. I'm afraid, however, that the Spirit's role has often been minimized within evangelicalism in recent decades—either in a preoccupation with human-centered techniques or in an overreaction to charismatic excesses. This tendency to look only to our own resources is not new. In 1879, Baptist pastor and theologian Hezekiah Harvey, writing about the pastor's inner life, expressed some instructions that apply to all believers:

> Ancient asceticism, in demanding for the ministry a hidden life of communion with God, gave voice not only to one of the profoundest intuitions of the Christian consciousness, but also to one of the clearest teachings of Scripture. The men who deal with spiritual things must themselves be spiritual. Our age, while rightly rejecting a perverted asceticism, is tending to the opposite error. It is intensely practical. "Action!" is its watchword. This

> practicalness often becomes mere narrowness and shallowness. It overlooks the profounder laws of the Christian life. Spiritual force comes from within, from the hidden life of God in the soul. It depends, not on mere outward activities, but on the divine energies acting through the human faculties, God working through the man, the Holy Ghost permeating, quickening all the powers of the preacher, and speaking by his voice to the souls of the people. The soul's secret power with God thus gives public power with men, and the mightiest influences of the pulpit often flow from a hidden spring in the solitude of the closet; for a sermon is not the mere utterance of man: there is in it a power more than human. Its vital force comes from the Holy Spirit. Jesus said: "It is not ye that speak, but the Spirit of your Father that speaketh in you" (Matt. x. 20). Its spiritual energy springs from something deeper than logic and rhetoric.[1]

Early in the disciples' ministry with Jesus, He illustrated their need to rely on His power for even the most ordinary tasks. Such an illustration deeply affected Simon Peter and some other disciples:

> When He had finished speaking, He said to Simon, "Put out into the deep water and let down your nets for a catch." Simon answered and said, "Master, we

> worked hard all night and caught nothing, but I will do as You say and let down the nets." When they had done this, they enclosed a great quantity of fish, and their nets began to break; so they signaled to their partners in the other boat for them to come and help them. And they came and filled both of the boats, so that they began to sink. But when Simon Peter saw that, he fell down at Jesus' feet, saying, "Go away from me Lord, for I am a sinful man!" For amazement had seized him and all his companions because of the catch of fish which they had taken. (Luke 5:4–9)

The disciples' need for supernatural resources and empowerment again was very apparent in the post-transfiguration story of Mark 9:14–29. That was the episode in which Jesus, with Peter, James, and John, came down from the mountain and encountered the other disciples with a crowd. The nine disciples had been unable to cast an evil spirit out of a man's son. Jesus had to step in and get rid of the unclean spirit. Later, the Lord told the disciples they could not depend solely on their own resources: "When He came into the house, His disciples began questioning Him privately, 'Why could we not drive it out?' And He said to them, 'This kind cannot come out by anything but prayer'" (vv. 28–29).

We can be precise and orthodox about every doctrinal fact, and we can exhibit a certain degree of willingness and ability to serve the Lord, but until we rely upon the Holy Spirit for wisdom and power, all our activities are ineffective. Without Him, we are like a new car with all the options and the shiniest of exteriors but no engine. It might look good, but it certainly won't run.

Jesus prepared His disciples to expect the outpouring of the Holy Spirit: "Gathering them together, He commanded them not to leave Jerusalem, but to wait for what the Father had promised, 'Which,' He said, 'you heard of from Me; for John baptized with water, but you will be baptized with the Holy Spirit not many days from now'" (Acts 1:4–5). The promise set forth in John 14—16 was about to be fulfilled.

The Baptism of the Holy Spirit

The tremendous public outpouring of the Holy Spirit at the Feast of Pentecost in Acts 2 is one of the great events in Scripture. It is memorable not only because extraordinary supernatural displays were evident, but also because it was a major turning point in God's program. Christ's church was born, and the disciples were fully equipped to begin the task of building it.

Evidence of the Spirit's Coming

Luke's words in Acts 2:1–4 are very familiar to any student of Scripture, but they can be and often are misinterpreted and misapplied. This passage is most readily understood if we simply read it as a historical presentation of the visible evidence of the Holy Spirit's coming. Such a reading will keep us from inserting elements that don't belong and from drawing invalid inferences concerning what happened on that momentous day.

Acts 2:1–4 describes the events at Pentecost in a concise, straightforward manner:

> When the day of Pentecost had come, they were all together in one place. And suddenly there came from heaven a noise like a violent rushing wind, and it filled the whole house where they were sitting. And there appeared to them tongues as of fire distributing themselves, and they rested on each one of them. And they were all filled with the Holy Spirit and began to speak with other tongues, as the Spirit was giving them utterance.

Luke did not mention anything about requirements the disciples fulfilled, exercises they completed, or prayers they offered. The events happened, not in response to the people's activities or persuasion, but strictly because of God's powerful initiative.

Because of the important spiritual truths the Feast of Pentecost pictured, God chose to bring the baptism of the Spirit right on that day. Pentecost was the Greek name for the Israelite Feast of Weeks (Ex. 34:22–23) or Feast of the Harvest (23:16). It involved the offering of the firstfruits of the grain harvest and was third in a sequence of feasts, after Passover and Unleavened Bread (which also required a firstfruits offering). In spiritual significance and meaning, these three feasts are often seen as parallels to Christ's death, His resurrection, and His sending of the Spirit. The time interval between each of these events at the end of Jesus' earthly life is the same as the time between each Old Testament feast, further strengthening the comparison. The coming of the Spirit to live within the apostles is the firstfruits of our final, future inheritance (2 Cor. 5:5; Eph. 1:13–14).[2]

Two physical phenomena accompanied the Spirit's arrival: the noise of a strong blowing wind and the appearance of fire-like tongues over the believers' heads. We know from experience that certain signs point to specific natural occurrences. Anyone who has grown up near the coasts of the southeastern or eastern United States or on the Great Plains, from Texas to Minnesota, knows that hurricanes and tornadoes are always accompanied by strong, noisy winds. The sound is frightening and unmistakable. God sovereignly chose to use audible and visual effects to let those gathered on Pentecost know that something special was happening.

The Lord Jesus had already compared the Holy Spirit with wind (John 3:8; see also Ezek. 37:9–14). In Acts 2:2 the word for wind does not mean merely a gentle breeze; it indicates a strong blast. There was no actual movement of air, but that was not the point. The key factor was the sound, and it was distinct and hard to miss. God used the noise to draw a large crowd to witness what He was doing.

The appearance of fire had much the same effect on the Pentecost witnesses as did the sound of the wind. The physical essence was not as important as the fire's spiritual meaning. The bright tongues over the believers' heads were not actual fire but supernatural indicators that God had sent His Spirit upon each one, without exception. The disciples needed to see that a significant event actually was happening—their spiritual senses could not comprehend it without some sovereignly supplied visual aid. God's use of the "tongues as of fire" is analogous to what He did when Jesus was baptized. He sent the Holy Spirit in the form of a dove to prove that Christ was indeed empowered and approved by the Father.

The final, amazing Pentecost phenomenon was the disciples' speaking in other languages. Most informed Christians know about the controversial issue of speaking in tongues that is associated with Acts 2:4. I have dealt with this issue in depth elsewhere,[3] so I will just comment briefly here. "Other tongues" were other known human languages, and the disciples displayed the ability to speak them to testify of God's glory and the Spirit's power. This gift is not ongoing for believers today and thus should not be expected to result from any striving to "receive the baptism of the Spirit."

None of the outward evidences of the Holy Spirit's coming in Acts 2 was the result of human ingenuity or manipulation. Everything was of God, from start to finish.

Effect of the Spirit's Coming

The miraculous evidences of the Holy Spirit's arrival quickly drew the attention of the crowds gathered in Jerusalem. Luke's continuing account in Acts 2 describes what happened: "Now there were Jews living in Jerusalem, devout men, from every nation under heaven. And when this sound occurred, the crowd came together, and were bewildered because each one of them was hearing them speak in his own language" (vv. 5–6).

Notice that between the noise and the languages, the noise is the evidence that first grabbed everyone's attention. The noise that sounded like high winds (v. 2) was not an average, everyday sound. It probably had some familiar characteristics, but it was the extreme decibel level that drew people away from what they were doing. Most of us have experienced that kind of distraction at some time. It may have been a nearby explosion, a low-flying aircraft, or a loud car wreck in our neighborhood. Any of those occurrences might cause us to investigate what happened. But such examples can only approximate what the Jewish pilgrims must have felt on the day of Pentecost.

It was a mind-boggling experience for those who responded to the supernatural sound. First there was surprise at the unusual noise, then there was absolute amazement and perplexity at hearing and understanding what some foreigners (the disciples from Galilee) were saying (Acts 2:7–8). But the disciples were not speaking in other people's languages pridefully or as a way just to attract attention to themselves. Instead, the Acts narrative says the crowd was impressed because "we hear them in our own tongues speaking of the mighty deeds of God" (v. 11). The Holy Spirit used such words of praise, from the Psalms and the books of Moses, to prepare many hearts to receive Peter's sermon, which was the climax of the day (vv. 14–47).

So much more could be written about the turning-point events in Acts 2, but the essential truth to convey is this: The baptism of the Spirit is a sovereign work. Everything that happened in Jerusalem on that most important of Pentecosts was orchestrated by the Father to make it clear that the Spirit's coming perfectly fit the divine timetable. Peter supported this truth at the outset of his great sermon when he quoted from the prophet Joel (Acts 2:16–17). No matter how incredible the events surrounding Pentecost may seem to our finite minds, and no matter how hard some would strive to give them a human explanation, there is no escaping the fact that all the credit belongs to God:

> For God has shut up all in disobedience that He
> may show mercy to all.

> Oh, the depth of the riches both of the wisdom and knowledge of God! How unsearchable are His judgments and unfathomable His ways! For who has known the mind of the Lord, or who became His counselor? Or who has first given to Him that it might be paid back to him again? For from Him and through Him and to Him are all things. To Him be the glory forever. Amen. (Rom. 11:32–36)

Reality of the Spirit's Coming

Just as Scripture gives us trustworthy proof that Pentecost was a sovereign miracle, God's Word also provides us with the best understanding of the present reality of Spirit baptism. In 1 Corinthians 12:13 the apostle Paul said, "For by one Spirit we were all baptized into one body, whether Jews or Greeks, whether slaves or free, and we were all made to drink of one Spirit." Paul was presenting two unifying concepts (he was originally dealing with the lack of unity in the Corinthian church), which provide a near-perfect commentary on what happened in the early part of Acts: All believers have been placed into the body of Christ in the same way, and all believers possess the same Holy Spirit.

In the phrase "by one Spirit," the apostle used the preposition *by* for a precise reason. *By* indicates the Holy Spirit was Christ's agent in bringing us into God's family. The Spirit does not act independently from Christ's work and bestow some sort of mystical baptism on certain believers. If the Spirit did work in such a separate manner, Paul would have likely used *of* rather than *by*. The Scripture really nowhere makes Spirit baptism the special possession of the Holy Spirit. (This makes it incorrect even to use the popular expression "baptism *of* the Holy Spirit.")

A careful reading of certain gospel passages supports Paul's opening words in 1 Corinthians 12:13. John the Baptist gave us this testimony in Mark and elsewhere: "After me One is coming who is mightier than I, and I am not fit to stoop down and untie the thong of His sandals. I baptized you with water; but He will baptize you with [by] the Holy Spirit" (Mark 1:7–8; see also Matt. 3:11–12; Luke 3:16; John 1:33–34). In each of these references, it is clear that Christ is actually the baptizer, *by means of* the Holy Spirit. Peter's sermon also verifies this truth in relation to Pentecost: "This Jesus God raised up again, to which we are all witnesses. Therefore having been exalted to the right hand of God, and having received from the Father the promise of the Holy Spirit, He has poured forth this which you both see and hear" (Acts 2:32–33).

Jesus and the Holy Spirit work together in the process of bringing us into Christ's body. It is unscriptural to think of spiritual baptism in two separate phases. We are not saved in Christ in one stage and then required to seek Spirit baptism in a second stage. Such is the common misconception of some professing Christians who would ask other Christians, "Have you received the baptism of the Holy Spirit?"

To make Spirit baptism a separate process is actually to tamper with the doctrine of salvation. Consider what Jesus said in John 7:37–39: "'If anyone is thirsty, let him come to Me and drink. He who believes in Me, as the Scripture said, "From his innermost being will flow rivers of living water."' But this He spoke of the Spirit, whom those who believed in Him were to receive." Here Christ is giving a straightforward invitation to believe and be saved. And all who heed this invitation will at the same time receive the Holy Spirit. So again we see that salvation and Spirit baptism are one process—if we are Christians, we will have the promised indwelling of the Holy Spirit.

The arrival of the Holy Spirit was indeed a most powerful demonstration of the sovereign actions of God. It should also be a constant reminder of the faithfulness and consistency of the triune God's working for our good and for His glory. Although the outpouring of the Spirit did not happen as the result of emotional actions or pleadings by the apostles—and it does not happen to us that way either—the Holy Spirit's presence and guidance gives believers a greater sense of joy, comfort, and assurance than anything else they will know. The apostle Paul prayed that the Ephesians would fully realize their privileges and benefits as ones placed by the Spirit into Christ's church (Eph. 3:14–21). Of course, that prayer is also a great source of encouragement to any who seek to walk on the Spirit-led pathway.

How can we summarize, in a practical way, the significance of the Holy Spirit's outpouring? Here is what the respected writer and theologian J. I. Packer wrote on the matter:

> We should not see the essence of this epoch-making event [Pentecost] in the tornado sound, the sight of human tongues afire over each person's head, and the gift of language (these were secondary matters, what we might call the trimmings). We

should see the essence of it, rather, in the fact that at nine o'clock that morning the Holy Spirit's new covenant ministry began, giving each disciple a clear understanding of Jesus' place in God's plan, a robust sense of identity and authority as Jesus' person in this world, and an unlimited boldness in proclaiming Jesus' power from his throne—the new elements that are so amazing in Peter's sermon when we recall what sort of man he had been before. Jesus had promised that when the Spirit came he would empower the disciples for witness (Acts 1:5, 8), and Luke evidently means us to see in Peter, whose failures he had diligently chronicled in his Gospel, a model instance of that promise being fulfilled. And he means us also to understand that this new covenant "gift of the Holy Spirit"—in other words, experiential enjoyment of this new ministry whereby the Spirit glorifies Jesus to, in, and through His people—is promised to all who repent and are baptized, from the moment their discipleship starts.[4]

6

THE SILENT SHEPHERD AT WORK FOR US

One of the great hymns of the Christian church expresses, as no theology text can, the marvelous way in which the Holy Spirit brings us into a right relationship with God. The final two stanzas of "And Can It Be?" reflect the feelings of the hymn's composer, Charles Wesley, not long after his conversion in the spring of 1738:

Long my imprisoned spirit lay
Fast bound in sin and nature's night.
Thine eye diffused a quick'ning ray:
I woke—the dungeon flamed with light!
My chains fell off, my heart was free,
I rose, went forth, and followed Thee.

No condemnation now I dread:
Jesus, and all in Him, is mine!
Alive in Him, my living Head,
And clothed in righteousness divine,
Bold I approach th'eternal throne,
And claim the crown, thru Christ my own.

This extraordinary sense of freedom from spiritual condemnation can and should belong to every person who knows and loves Christ. Romans 8:1–2 says, "Therefore there is now no condemnation for those who are in Christ Jesus. For the law of the Spirit of life in Christ Jesus has set you free from the law of sin and of death." Here again the apostle Paul was reminding believers of that clear line of difference between the gospel of the new covenant and the law of the old covenant. In chapters 3 and 4 we saw how our Silent Shepherd, the Spirit, delineates many of these differences and proves the superiority of the new covenant. Now we'll examine more specifically what the Spirit does for us to help us enjoy the richness of new covenant life in Christ.

He Frees Us from Sin and Death

The moment we become Christians, we are freed from the power of sin and death. It's as if one minute we were prisoners in solitary confinement at a maximum-security penitentiary, and the next minute we were pardoned and released simultaneously. Suddenly we would no longer be confined to a small area, we would no longer have to eat prison food or wear prison clothing, we would no longer have our communication with the outside world severely restricted—we would be free from all the rules, regulations, and deprivations typically associated with prison life. This is the kind of spiritual transformation pictured by Charles Wesley in his hymn, and it happens only by the Spirit-energized power of the gospel, which Paul called "the Spirit of life in Christ Jesus" (Rom. 8:2).

Jesus was very confident in this liberating power of the gospel when He declared in John 5:24: "Truly, truly, I say to you, he who hears My word, and believes Him who sent Me, has eternal life, and does not come into judgment, but has passed out of death into life" (see also John 8:32–36). The Holy Spirit, through Scripture, wants to leave no doubt that each and every person He has sovereignly placed in Christ He has also freed from the power of sin and death. The apostle Paul wrote,

> Now if we have died with Christ, we believe that we shall also live with Him, knowing that Christ, having been raised from the dead, is never to die again; death no longer is master over Him. For the death that He died, He died to sin once for all; but the life that He lives, He lives to God. Even so consider yourselves to be dead to sin, but alive to God in Christ Jesus. (Rom. 6:8–11)

At the end of this passage Paul exhorted believers to take an active role in appropriating this freedom from sin that is theirs. We must continually remind ourselves that we are dead to sin and alive to God (Col. 3:3–10). It is a joyous reassurance to know that the

Holy Spirit enables us habitually to claim victory over sin and live in obedience to God.

He Enables Us to Fulfill the Law

A second vital work the Holy Spirit does for believers—also in connection with salvation—is He enables us to fulfill God's law. This is one of the first positive consequences of God's gift of the new birth, which agrees with the assertion of the ancient church theologian Augustine: "Saving grace was given that the Law might be fulfilled."

When a Christian is active in fulfilling the law of God, he or she is not merely demonstrating some painstaking, external conformity to a divine code of ethics. The believer's obedience to God's commands is the result of the Spirit's dwelling inside him or her. This indwelling produces first of all the proper attitudes: love, joy, peace, patience, kindness, goodness, faithfulness, gentleness, self-control—all are aspects of the Spirit's fruit (Gal. 5:22–23). These attitudes then result in righteous actions that please God.

The apostle Paul understood well God's sovereign plan for us after salvation:

> For by grace you have been saved through faith; and that not of yourselves, it is the gift of God; not as a result of works, so that no one may boast. For we are His workmanship, created in Christ Jesus for good works, which God prepared beforehand so that we would walk in them. (Eph. 2:8–10; see also Titus 2:14)

These familiar verses once again bring into focus the truth that salvation and discipleship are inseparable. If we have been transformed by the Spirit's power, that fact will be evident in the way we live and serve the Lord (Matt. 7:20–21; James 2:17–26). Our lifestyles won't be perfect, because we are still sinners, but the Holy Spirit is with us to assist us to fulfill the law of God.

He Gives Us Our Identity

One of the results to a Christian who fulfills God's law is acquiring a spiritual identity: Such a sense of identity is far more important than the sense of individual, physical identity we all take for granted but don't fully understand. Only the discovery of the DNA molecule within the past sixty years has proved more clearly than ever before the unique physical identity of all individuals. Researchers first discovered that DNA carries the genetic information in all living systems and provides the most fundamental explanation of genetic laws. More recently, highly skilled technicians assisted scientists in putting knowledge about DNA to practical use. The most publicized is DNA fingerprinting, a technique that compares the DNA marker information of one piece with that found in a sample of another. If the information matches, it is fairly certain the two pieces came from the same person. This fingerprinting has been hailed as more reliable than traditional fingerprinting in proving a person's identity or determining a child's mother or father.

Discoveries about DNA and genetic identity may have been big news in the scientific world, but that news is nothing compared to the truth God established long ago concerning spiritual identity: In

John 3:6, as He was presenting the gospel to Nicodemus, our Lord said, "That which is born of the flesh is flesh, and that which is born of the Spirit is spirit." Jesus established the basic distinction between one who is born again and one who is not. The apostle Paul gave this same essential definition of a Christian in Romans 8:9: "However, you are not in the flesh but in the Spirit, if indeed the Spirit of God dwells in you. But if anyone does not have the Spirit of Christ, he does not belong to Him." In other words, anyone who is a Christian will know the indwelling presence of the Holy Spirit in his or her life.

Romans 8:9 is also a sober reminder that if our lives do not show evidence of the Spirit's fruit, He is not living in us, and we are not Christians. If you are struggling right now to know if you belong to Christ, remember what Paul told the Corinthians in 2 Corinthians 13:5, "Test yourselves to see if you are in the faith; examine yourselves! Or do you not recognize this about yourselves, that Jesus Christ is in you—unless indeed you fail the test?" This self-examination does not have to be a gloomy, morbid look inside yourself. Instead, it may simply consist of a series of questions you ask yourself, such as: Have I experienced the leading, encouraging, assuring work of the Holy Spirit in my life? Have I experienced any aspects of the fruit of the Spirit? Have I known and shown love for other members of the body of Christ? Has my heart longed to commune with God in prayer? Do I have a love for God's Word, and are its truths clear and compelling to me? If you can remember times when the answer to any of these questions was clearly yes, then you are most likely a Christian.

The Spirit of God is still indwelling you even if all the good qualities just mentioned are not now present in your life. You may not sense the Spirit's presence or feel like following His guidance every moment, but His presence is dependent on God's promises, not our feelings.

He Points Us to Christ

Believers must have a clear and correct understanding of what it means to have Christ at the center of their lives. The author of the letter to the Hebrews said, "Let us run with endurance the race that is set before us, fixing our eyes on Jesus, the author and perfecter of faith, who for the joy set before Him endured the cross, despising the shame, and has sat down at the right hand of the throne of God" (Heb. 12:1–2). It is one of the Holy Spirit's key ministries to draw us to Christ initially, and it is also the Spirit's work to keep us focused on Christ, exalting Christ, and glorifying Christ.

In the gospel of John, Jesus Himself twice stated that the Holy Spirit directs our attention to Christ:

- "When the Helper comes, whom I will send to you from the Father, that is the Spirit of truth who proceeds from the Father, He will testify about Me" (John 15:26).

- "He will glorify Me, for He will take of Mine and will disclose it to you. All things that the Father has are Mine; therefore I said that He takes of Mine and will disclose it to you" (John 16:14–15).

The Holy Spirit places the spotlight on Christ by bearing witness, which is an important and frequently mentioned truth in John's gospel. John wrote of six other persons and things that testify about Christ: God the Father (5:31–37; 8:18), Christ Himself (8:14, 18), the works of Jesus (5:36; 10:25), Scripture (5:39), John the Baptist (1:6–8), and various human witnesses (4:39; 12:17; 15:27). Commentator Leon Morris put the significance of bearing witness, or giving one's testimony, into perspective:

> This emphasis on testimony should not be overlooked. There is a legal air about it. Testimony is a serious matter and it is required to substantiate the truth of a matter.... This bearing of witness was not an end in itself. Behind it was the purpose "that all might believe through him."[1]

In 1 Corinthians 12:3, the apostle Paul gave further support to the Spirit's ministry of exalting Christ: "No one can say, 'Jesus is Lord,' except by the Holy Spirit." It is always the Holy Spirit's desire to lift up and underscore the lordship of Christ. The Spirit wants the church to see Christ as Lord so that all who are members will recognize His authority and submit to His will (Phil. 2:9–13). He also testifies that Jesus is Lord so that we might see Christ's model of beauty, purity, and righteousness and want to be like Him (Matt. 11:28–30; 16:24; 1 Peter 2:21).

Just as the power and wisdom of the Holy Spirit are absolutely necessary for anyone to realize his or her sinful condition, to turn from that condition, and to embrace the finished work of Jesus' death and resurrection, so the Spirit is necessary for us to realize Christ's lordship and our ongoing duty of discipleship. It is so foolish for us to attempt to perform that duty by focusing on ourselves and our many activities. But as new covenant believers, we must remember that there is a better way. We are not limited as Moses and the Israelites were, with veiled faces and darkened understandings regarding God's glory. The Holy Spirit instead opens the way for us to see more and more of Christ's glory:

> But whenever a person turns to the Lord, the veil is taken away. Now the Lord is the Spirit, and where the Spirit of the Lord is, there is liberty. But we all, with unveiled face, beholding as in a mirror the glory of the Lord, are being transformed into the same image from glory to glory, just as from the Lord, the Spirit. (2 Cor. 3:16–18)

He Leads Us into God's Will

One of the most practical ministries the Holy Spirit performs for us is leading us into God's will. This is not new or surprising—the Lord clearly stated the fact of the Spirit's guidance along with the promise of the new covenant: "I will put My Spirit within you and cause you to walk in My statutes, and you will be careful to observe My ordinances" (Ezek. 36:27). But even long before the prophet Ezekiel's promise, God's Spirit was active in the Old Testament in leading and guiding His people:

> Then His people remembered the days of old, of Moses. Where is He who brought them up out of the sea with the shepherds of His flock? Where is He who put His Holy Spirit in the midst of them, who caused His glorious arm to go at the right hand of Moses, who divided the waters before them to make for Himself an everlasting name, who led them through the depths? Like the horse in the wilderness, they did not stumble; as the cattle which go down into the valley, the Spirit of the LORD gave them rest. So You led Your people, to make for Yourself a glorious name. (Isa. 63:11–14)

As God showed the way during Old Testament times, we can be sure that His Spirit has done and will continue to do the same thing in this era. The book of Acts contains two remarkable examples of how the Spirit led in key decision making. First there was the selection by the Antioch church leaders of Paul and Barnabas to be missionaries: "While they were ministering to the Lord and fasting, the Holy Spirit said, 'Set apart for Me Barnabas and Saul for the work to which I have called them.' Then, when they had fasted and prayed and laid their hands on them, they sent them away" (Acts 13:2–3).

Then there was the occasion of the Jerusalem Council: a discussion among church leaders on how the Jewish Christians and the many new Gentile converts should relate and what requirements the Jewish-led church should place on the new believers. This is how the apostles and elders of the Jerusalem church concluded their letter of recommendation that was carried to the largely Gentile Antioch church: "For it seemed good to the Holy Spirit and to us to lay upon you no greater burden than these essentials: that you abstain from things sacrificed to idols and from blood and from things strangled and from fornication; if you keep yourselves free from such things, you will do well. Farewell" (Acts 15:28–29).

The letter in Acts 15 resulted from a Spirit-led consensus among the leaders. In their hearts, the apostles and elders knew they had made the right decision, because they had the confidence that their conclusion was from the mind of the Spirit. We can have that same confidence. Romans 8:14 says, "For all who are being led by the Spirit of God, these are sons of God." If we are believers who are sensitive to the Spirit, spend regular time in the Word, and seek to obey the Lord, He will lead us into His will (see Ps. 119:105).

He Ministers to Us through Others

At this point it might be easy to think, *If the Holy Spirit dwells in me and He is sufficient, then I have all I need.* Such reasoning is true, but it needs clarification. Because we have not yet reached complete sanctification, the sufficiency of the Holy Spirit is not always a reality in our lives. Therefore, one of the things God uses to exhort, correct, and encourage us is the Spirit's ministry from and through other believers.

Scripture is crystal clear in its command that believers are to associate with one another. The author of Hebrews wrote, "Let us hold fast the confession of our hope without wavering, for He who promised is faithful; and let us consider how to stimulate one another to love and good deeds, not forsaking our own assembling together, as is the habit of some, but encouraging one another; and all the more as you see the day drawing near" (Heb. 10:23–25). This passage reminds us that God wants Christians who are consistent and faithful—those who won't waver in their profession of faith. One of the primary ways this can be realized is for believers to think seriously of how they can stimulate one another to love and do good deeds. But that can't occur if we do not gather together regularly.

The God-ordained framework in which we can meet together and most effectively encourage one another toward godliness is the church. Several times in his letters the apostle Paul used the analogy of the human body to describe how relationships within the church, Christ's body, are designed to work. For example, in Romans 12:4–6, he wrote, "For just as we have many members in one body and all the members do not have the same function, so we, who are many, are one body in Christ, and individually members one of another. Since we have gifts that differ according to the grace given to us, each of us is to exercise them accordingly." Paul then presented the familiar list of spiritual gifts, including service, teaching, exhortation, and giving (see also 1 Cor. 12; Eph. 4:4, 11–12).

Spiritual gifts are nothing more than the loving channels through which the Holy Spirit ministers to the body of Christ. First Corinthians 12:7 and 11 summarize well the purpose of the gifts: "To each one is given the manifestation of the Spirit for the common good.… But one and the same Spirit works all these things, distributing to each one individually just as He wills." These verses reveal once again that the Holy Spirit sovereignly works for us in many varied and beneficial ways—the ministry of spiritual gifts is all His, and every manifestation is designed to build up the church (Eph. 4:12).

What is truly remarkable about the Holy Spirit's ministry through believers is that they become extensions of the Spirit's voice, much as they become ambassadors for Christ when they minister the gospel to others. This fact ought to encourage us toward greater holiness as we seek to use our spiritual gifts and insights to help others. It also ought to make us more sensitive to the stimulus of the Spirit's correction when others lovingly come alongside and minister to us (Gal. 6:1; Phil. 2:3–4; Col. 3:12–13).

Paul quite plainly connected love and the Holy Spirit in Romans 5:5, which says in part, "the love of God has been poured out within our hearts through the Holy Spirit who was given to us" (see also Rom. 15:30; 2 Cor. 6:6; Col. 1:8). The association between love and the Holy Spirit is most strongly made in 1 Corinthians 13. This chapter, set right in the middle of Paul's section on spiritual gifts, gives us all the guidance we'll ever need as we allow the Spirit to use us in reaching out to others. Paul ascribed the highest prominence to the attribute of love in the believer's life as he concluded chapter 13 with these familiar words: "But now faith, hope, love, abide these three; but the greatest of these is love" (v. 13).

He Empowers Us for Service

During the holiday gift-giving season, three of the most dreaded words we can read, along with "some assembly required," are "batteries not included." What parents haven't felt frustrated when, late on Christmas Eve while wrapping toys for their children, they unexpectedly find that a special toy did not come with the batteries needed to operate it. The harried parents are then faced with the prospect of either not having a workable toy the next day or having to venture out at the last minute to buy some batteries.

Isn't it wonderful that all the gifts and abilities from the Holy Spirit are not like Christmas toys without batteries? When He gives us new birth and seals our adoption as God's children, He also provides all the power we will ever need to live the Christian life and use our spiritual gifts effectively to build up other believers.

When we say the Spirit has all the power we will ever need, that implies a huge, infinite supply of strength—more than any human-centered source of wisdom, no matter how intellectual; and greater than any high-tech power source, no matter how state of the art. The apostle Paul understood this principle very well: "Now to Him who is able to do far more abundantly beyond all that we ask or think, according to the power that works within us" (Eph. 3:20). He had just prayed that the Ephesian Christians would "be strengthened with power through His Spirit in the inner man" (v. 16) and thereby realize the full extent of the riches of God's glory in their lives. There was no doubt in Paul's mind that God and the Holy Spirit are able to do far more than most believers ever conceive. So many of us never get beyond the first phrase of verse 20: "to Him who is able." Unfortunately, we tend to limit the extent of the Spirit's work in and through us.

Paul not only knew intellectually about the Holy Spirit's infinite power source, but he also experienced it in his ministry. Here's what he wrote in the face of extremely difficult challenges that stretched him to the limit, both physically and spiritually:

> We have this treasure in earthen vessels, so that the surpassing greatness of the power will be of God [and the Holy Spirit] and not from ourselves; we are afflicted in every way, but not crushed; perplexed, but not despairing; persecuted, but not forsaken; struck down, but not destroyed; always carrying about in the body the dying of Jesus, so that the life of Jesus also may be manifested in our body. For we who live are constantly being delivered over to death for Jesus' sake, so that the life of Jesus also may be manifested in our mortal flesh. So death works in us, but life in you.... Therefore we do not lose heart, but though our outer man is decaying, yet our inner man is being renewed day by day. (2 Cor. 4:7–12, 16)

The source of Paul's inner strength to persevere through such circumstances could be none other than the Holy Spirit. And the same Spirit is our source of strength, no matter how challenging the situations we face. We can be hampered without being frustrated, puzzled without being in despair, persecuted without having to stand alone, knocked down but never knocked out, dying in our bodies but alive in our hearts, and facing physical death to bring people spiritual life. Even though our outer man is wearing down and being torn up, our inner man is being renewed with fresh strength every day from the Holy Spirit.

He Intercedes for Us before God

There is one more aspect of the Holy Spirit's ministry on our behalf—He intercedes for us before God. The apostle Paul addressed this part of the Spirit's work:

> In the same way the Spirit also helps our weakness; for we do not know how to pray as we should, but the Spirit Himself intercedes for us with groanings too deep for words; and He who searches the hearts knows what the mind of the Spirit is, because He intercedes for the saints according to the will of God. (Rom. 8:26–27)

Those verses are part of Paul's culmination of a key section of Romans 8. That passage describes the profound, extended yearning—Paul called it groaning—that the whole creation, all Christians, and now the Holy Spirit have for the glorious day when we will be freed from the corrupting effects of sin. In a wonderfully comforting fashion, the Spirit is confirming to our hearts that He is on our side through this life, shepherding us toward our heavenly destination.

It is also comforting to know that the Holy Spirit is on our side in an active way, working out a secure salvation for us as part of God's overall sovereign plan. He once again proves to us that He is present, just as Christ promised, and that He and the Son are in full agreement in interceding for believers (Rom. 8:34; Heb. 7:25). Jesus, for example, interceded for His followers even before He ascended to the right hand of His Father: "Simon, Simon, behold, Satan has demanded permission to sift you like wheat; but I have prayed for you, that your faith may not fail; and you, when once you have turned again, strengthen your brothers" (Luke 22:31–32). Jesus' intercession was perfectly in accord with God's plan that, even though they are secure in their salvation if they have been truly converted, believers still need the Son and the Spirit to constantly work out that security (Phil. 1:6; 1 John 1:9). And that preserving work is not at all contradictory to Paul's command in Philippians 2:12 to "work out your salvation with fear and trembling." The very next verse provides the balance: "for it is God who is at work in you" (v. 13).

We would be at a loss, an eternal loss, if God did not provide this ministry of intercession by the Spirit. He intercedes for us with divine sighs as He prays to the Father for our full glorification. The Spirit understands our sinful and weak flesh and knows that we don't know how to pray properly for ourselves or sustain our spiritual lives.

But what are these sighs or groanings that Paul mentioned in Romans 8:26? Certainly they do not verify, as some would say, any kind of ecstatic "speaking in tongues" by believers. They are more accurately communications between the Spirit and the Father that transcend human language. The sighs and groans are in that sense silent to us—we can't put them into words and therefore we can't know exactly what the Spirit is saying, but we can know that He is praying for us. Commentator John Murray supplied these helpful summarizing insights:

> Since they are the intercessions of the Holy Spirit, they always meet with the understanding and approval of God. They are agreeable to his will as are the intercessions of Christ at the right hand of God. The encouragement extended to the people of God is that the unuttered groans are the index to the fact that God does "exceeding abundantly above all that we ask or think" (Eph. 3:20) and that not our infirmity of understanding and request is the measure of God's grace but the knowledge, wisdom, and love of the Holy Spirit.[2]

Romans 7:18–19 says, "For I know that nothing good dwells in me, that is, in my flesh; for the willing is present in me, but the doing of the good is not. For the good that I want, I do not do, but I practice the very evil that I do not want." Paul here described his continual, daily struggle to overcome sin and persevere in righteousness. The apostle knew he could not win the struggle on his own, and God revealed to him the great truths of life and freedom in Christ and the Holy Spirit (Rom. 8). We have drawn from just a portion of these in reminding ourselves that we also are utterly dependent on the Holy Spirit to minister to us and assist us with our Christian walk. It is easy enough for most of us to remember that the Spirit had a vital role in bringing us to faith, but we so often forget about or ignore our ongoing need for the Spirit to help us live that faith daily. Commentator Arthur W. Pink recalled this fact for us when he wrote,

As the Christian owes his new life, or nature, to the Spirit, so by His power alone can it be vigorous and flourishing. Only by His strengthening of the heart are we delivered from being engrossed in the things around us, and our earthbound affections are drawn to things above. He it is who creates the desire for Christ, who shows us the things of Christ, who causes us to make Him the grand subject of our spiritual meditations. Only by the supernatural quickening of the Spirit can we be girded for that extraordinary effort of mind if we are to be "able to comprehend … and to know the love of Christ which passeth knowledge." And beyond any doubt, only by the operations and influences of the gracious Spirit may we be "filled with all the fullness of God." We are to daily seek from Him that quickening, enablement, and girding.[3]

7

A SCRIPTURAL PATH FOR THE SPIRITUAL WALK

The Bible is filled with examples of people who succumbed to the ways of the flesh rather than the commands of God and His Spirit. Such lapses were not always indicative of the person's general lifestyle and usual heart attitude, but yielding to the flesh in crucial situations always had negative consequences, which were often long-term. Think of Moses and Aaron in the wilderness of Zin where, rather than speak to the rock at Meribah for water as God commanded, they were impatient with Him and Moses struck the rock with his staff (Num. 20:6–13). As a result of their disobedience, the Lord denied them entrance into the Promised Land. Or consider what happened to King Saul when he took matters into his own hands concerning the burnt offering at Gilgal (1 Sam. 13:8–14; see also 15:3–31). Because Saul disobeyed God and did not wait for Samuel, the Lord removed him as king.

The story of brothers Jacob and Esau and the issue of Esau's birthright is another striking example of what can happen when believers and professing believers follow their fleshly instincts instead of God's principles. The episode began in Genesis 25:

> Now Isaac loved Esau, because he had a taste for game, but Rebekah loved Jacob. When Jacob had cooked stew, Esau came in from the field and he was famished; and Esau said to Jacob, "Please let me have a swallow of that red stuff there, for I am famished." Therefore his name was called Edom. But Jacob said, "First sell me your birthright." Esau said, "Behold I am about to die; so of what use is the birthright to me?" And Jacob said, "First swear to me"; so he swore to him, and sold his birthright to Jacob. Then Jacob gave Esau bread and lentil stew; and he ate and drank, and rose and went on his way. Thus Esau despised his birthright. (vv. 28–34)

The story of the birthright concludes in Genesis 27 with Jacob's deception, which secured his father Isaac's blessing for himself rather than for his older brother, Esau. The result of the lost inheritance was most bitter for Esau:

> Esau said to his father, "Do you have only one blessing, my father? Bless me, even me also, O my father." So Esau lifted his voice and wept. Then Isaac his father answered and said to him, "Behold, away

> from the fertility of the earth shall be your dwelling, and away from the dew of heaven from above. By your sword you shall live, and your brother you shall serve; but it shall come about when you become restless, that you shall break his yoke from your neck." So Esau bore a grudge against Jacob because of the blessing with which his father had blessed him; and Esau said to himself, "The days of mourning for my father are near; then I will kill my brother Jacob." (vv. 38–41)

Both brothers deserve some of the blame for what happened in this story, but in the long run Esau receives more blame. The writer to the Hebrews even cited him as a notorious example of the sort of "spirituality" to avoid: "See to it that no one comes short of the grace of God; that no root of bitterness springing up causes trouble, and by it many be defiled; that there be no immoral or godless person like Esau, who sold his own birthright for a single meal. For you know that even afterwards, when he desired to inherit the blessing, he was rejected, for he found no place for repentance, though he sought for it with tears" (Heb. 12:15–17). We can properly infer from Hebrews that Esau became apostate and therefore forfeited all his opportunities to get right with God.

The point for new covenant believers is simply this: We must shun the sinful expediency of substituting fleshly methods for spiritual means as we deal with life's challenges. Those of us who claim to know Christ and say we want to honor and serve Him must genuinely submit to Him and walk by the Spirit.

"Walk by the Spirit"

In Galatians 5:16, the apostle Paul issued this crucial command to the church at Galatia: "But I say, walk by the Spirit, and you will not carry out the desire of the flesh." This command is the baseline truth for how all believers should live day by day. Because life's problems, anxieties, and difficulties are so often caused by our flesh, the remedy for all these troubles is to defeat the lust of the flesh by walking in the Holy Spirit. Paul's imperative to us is not just pious and hollow rhetoric, either. The apostle John knew this and later gave us additional, solid incentive to overcome our flesh: "The world is passing away, and also its lusts; but the one who does the will of God lives forever" (1 John 2:17).

The Greek word for "walk" in Galatians 5:16 is a progressive present tense command with continuity, which could be translated literally "keep on continually walking." The basic idea is that the Christian life unfolds one day at a time. Walking is therefore a very picturesque metaphor that tells us we are to live one step at a time, as a matter of habit and routine. The Holy Spirit is already in us (Rom. 8:9; 1 Cor. 6:19) and working on our behalf. Our task is simply to respond and submit moment by moment, step by step, day by day according to His empowering and guiding.

A Pattern for the Spiritual Walk

The abstract command to walk by the Spirit sounds easy enough. But as with so many things in life, the challenge comes in carrying out what we know is true. For example, a basketball coach may diagram a play at the end of a close game. He hopes the play will result in a game-winning basket for his team, but unless his players execute the plan, which will be vigorously opposed by the other team, it will fail and the game will be lost. In the spiritual battle arena, the opposition comes from the flesh, which is implied in Galatians 5:16 and spelled out more clearly in verse 17: "For the flesh sets its desire against the Spirit, and the Spirit against the flesh; for these are in opposition to one another, so that you may not do the things that you please." In this arena it is even more imperative to know the biblical pattern for walking by the Spirit and how we can practically and effectively follow that pattern.[1]

Meditating on God's Word

Practically speaking, the first major piece in the pattern for the spiritual walk is a diligent and daily intake of God's Word. Many familiar verses attest to the importance of Scripture (Josh. 1:8; Pss. 19:7–11; 119:97–105; John 8:31–32; Rom. 15:4; Col. 3:16; 2 Tim. 2:15; 3:16–17; Heb. 4:12; 2 Peter 1:21), but one passage well suited for our discussion here—and not usually thought of in relation to the significance of the Word—is Psalm 1:1–3:

> How blessed is the man who does not walk in the counsel of the wicked, nor stand in the path of sinners, nor sit in the seat of scoffers! But his delight is in the law [Word] of the LORD, and in His law he meditates day and night. He will be like a tree firmly planted by streams of water, which yields its fruit in its season and its leaf does not wither; and in whatever he does, he prospers.

The psalmist mentioned a crucial element of Scripture intake: meditation. It is that one component that helps us seal to our hearts the content of God's Word, which we may initially just hear or read. Donald Whitney offered us this additional, useful insight on the value of meditation:

> Meditation goes beyond hearing, reading, studying, and even memorizing as a means of taking in God's Word. A simple analogy would be a cup of tea. You are the cup of hot water and the intake of Scripture is represented by the tea bag. Hearing God's Word is like one dip of the tea bag into the cup. Some of the tea's flavor is absorbed by the water, but not as much as would occur with a more thorough soaking of the bag. In this analogy, reading, studying, and memorizing God's Word are represented by additional plunges of the tea bag into the cup. The more frequently the tea enters the water, the more effect it has. Meditation, however, is like immersing the bag completely and letting it steep until all the rich tea flavor has been extracted and the hot water is thoroughly tinctured reddish brown.... True success is promised to those who meditate on God's Word, who think deeply on Scripture, not just at one time each day, but at moments throughout the day and night. They meditate so much that Scripture saturates their conversation. The fruit

> of their meditation is action. They do what they find written in God's Word and as a result God prospers their way and grants success to them.[2]

Therefore, as you take in the Word and meditate on it, you place yourself in a position where the Holy Spirit can most effectively help you walk as He wants you to walk.

A Heart Fixed on God

In addition to the importance of regular Scripture meditation, we must have our minds fixed on God if we are going to walk by the Spirit. The psalmist said this: "My heart is fixed, O God, my heart is fixed: I will sing and give praise" (Ps. 57:7 KJV). The New Testament also exhorts us about the importance of having our minds right and focusing on God. The apostle Paul gave this familiar imperative: "Do not be conformed to this world, but be transformed by the renewing of your mind, so that you may prove what the will of God is, that which is good and acceptable and perfect" (Rom. 12:2; see also Col. 3:2).

Of course, the next logical question is "How do we discipline our minds so they might be renewed and focused on God?" Writer and Bible teacher Dan DeHaan offered these practical and instructive insights, which fit well with Paul's admonition and the Old Testament proverb "as he [any person] thinks within himself, so he is" (Prov. 23:7):

> Mind-preoccupation will determine our goals, our enjoyment of reality, and our ability to affect other

> people's lives for the better. In order for Christlike behavior to be a way of life, there must be a preoccupation with "things above." That is not a dreamy kind of thing. It is the conscious worship of God's character that conforms us to what we worship. We always become what we worship. That is a law within even earthly relationships. What you bow down before, you become enamored with. Some people ponder and brood over their past victories or failures. They become past-conscious. Their day begins with the past. As a result, they can never really be what they should be right now, for this moment. Other people are preoccupied with position, possessions, or pleasure. They actually worship those things. Whether they know it or not, those are the things that control their thoughts throughout the day. They are becoming what they worship.
>
> Obviously, if we choose to worship that which is passing away, we reap the fruit of an equally unstable mind and character. Find me a worshiper of God, and I will show you a stable man with his mind in control, ready to meet the present hour with refreshment from above.[3]

People who have their minds renewed and fixed on God will indeed walk by the Spirit, because they worship God "in spirit and truth" (John 4:24).

Commune with God in Prayer

The next component in the pattern of the spiritual walk is communion with God in prayer. First Peter 4:7 commands all believers to "be of sound judgment and sober spirit for the purpose of prayer." Oftentimes when I'm in the Word, I don't know where my Bible study ends and my meditation begins, or where my meditation ends and my prayer begins. It becomes very much a seamless process in which I take in Scripture, meditate on it, and ask the Lord for help with those parts that I don't understand. I'm sure the experience is similar for many other believers who daily and weekly seek to be faithful.

Prayer is really an indispensable ingredient for any Christian who wants to walk by the Spirit. The moment-by-moment aspect of walking spiritually can be greatly supported and strengthened by a biblical attitude of prayer, an attitude that reflects the truth of 1 Thessalonians 5:17, "Pray without ceasing."[4]

Cameron V. Thompson drew directly from Scripture for this straightforward example that emphasizes the necessity of prayer:

> The secret of all failure is prayerlessness.... Prayerlessness is a disaster. Someone has said, "God froze Jacob by night and consumed him with drought in the day" (see Gen. 31:40), but twenty years passed before he would utter a word of prayer. When he did pray, he marvelously got in God's way trying to answer his own prayers (Gen. 32:9–20). It was only at Jabbok (the place of emptying) that he learned the secret of prevailing with God. For there

> he was emptied of all his natural strength and was wounded, lest he do anything else but cling to God all his life. "Jacob wrestling only failed; Jacob clinging soon prevailed."[5]

The example of Jacob wrestling with God ought to remind us once more that we cannot successfully follow the pattern of the spiritual walk if we rely on our own strength. The writer of Proverbs gave this familiar but sound advice: "Trust in the LORD with all your heart and do not lean on your own understanding. In all your ways acknowledge Him, and He will make your paths straight. Do not be wise in your own eyes; fear the LORD and turn away from evil" (Prov. 3:5–7). The New Testament is also clear regarding our task of walking on the Spirit's level. The apostle Peter reminded his readers of the wonderful advantages they had because of their position in Christ (2 Peter 1:1–3) and then went on to outline how they ought to live:

> Now for this very reason also, applying all diligence, in your faith supply moral excellence, and in your moral excellence, knowledge, and in your knowledge, self-control, and in your self-control, perseverance, and in your perseverance, godliness, and in your godliness, brotherly kindness, and in your brotherly kindness, love. For if these qualities are yours and are increasing, they render you neither useless nor unfruitful in the true knowledge of our Lord Jesus Christ. (2 Peter 1:5–8)

Peter had already admonished the readers of his first letter about their basic obligation as believers: "Beloved, I urge you as aliens and strangers to abstain from fleshly lusts which wage war against the soul" (1 Peter 2:11; see also Rom. 13:14). All of these statements taken together reinforce for us the image of walking on the narrow, long-distance path of discipleship (1 Peter 2:11 in the New King James Version uses the more picturesque "sojourners and pilgrims," which is perhaps more parallel with the spiritual-walk imagery). The point is, if we are living as disciples and faithfully cultivating obedience to the Lord (1 Peter 1:22), we will be following the pattern of the spiritual walk.

Ministering to One Another by the Spirit

It is indisputable that the Holy Spirit is sufficient to meet all our needs and supply us with all the spiritual means and materials to live as disciples of Jesus Christ. But it is also obvious that we often fail to walk by the Spirit as consistently as we would like or God would expect. The mere fact of sin in our lives is enough to prove our inconsistency (1 John 1:8–9; see also James 2:10; 3:2). The apostle Paul is an excellent example for us of one who understood the initial effect and continuing role of sin in our lives (see Rom. 7; 1 Tim. 1:15–16). He knew, therefore, that it would not always be easy to live the Christian life, but he also knew the value of perseverance. His words to the Philippians ought never to grow old:

> Not that I have already obtained it [the resurrection] or have already become perfect, but I press

> on so that I may lay hold of that for which also I was laid hold of by Christ Jesus. Brethren, I do not regard myself as having laid hold of it yet; but one thing I do: forgetting what lies behind and reaching forward to what lies ahead, I press on toward the goal for the prize of the upward call of God in Christ Jesus. Let us therefore, as many as are perfect, have this attitude; and if in anything you have a different attitude, God will reveal that also to you; however, let us keep living by that same standard to which we have attained.
>
> Brethren, join in following my example, and observe those who walk according to the pattern you have in us. (Phil. 3:12–17)

Because the believer's life is more of a marathon than a sprint, and because of our sinful inconsistency, it is difficult to walk by the Spirit all by ourselves. Even if the Holy Spirit is all-sufficient, we still need one another. That's just reality, as we pointed out in chapter 6. There we saw how the Spirit can minister to us through other Christians. Now I want you to see how our spiritual walk should encourage others.

Pick Up and Restore Others

It is often hard in our isolated, individualized Western cultures for us to appreciate the need we have for one another. It is easy for us, especially in the United States, to get entrenched in such individual patterns that we do not get close enough to others to discover their needs. The real problem with such a lifestyle is that it often spills over into the church and affects the way we minister—or don't minister—to others. It is certainly not the philosophy Paul had in mind when he planted and nurtured New Testament churches. His letters to the churches outline a better way.

Galatians 6:1–6, one of the key "one another" passages in the New Testament, flows right out of Paul's exhortation to believers to shun the deeds of the flesh, cultivate the fruit of the Spirit, and walk by the Spirit (5:16–26). God never intended for our spiritual walk to be an end in itself. Instead, He wants us to walk in a way that will have a positive influence on other believers and help purify and build up the church.

Galatians 6:1 contains the first element of how our spiritual walk should minister to others: "Brethren, even if anyone is caught in any trespass, you who are spiritual, restore such a one in a spirit of gentleness; each one looking to yourself, so that you too will not be tempted." We are to pick up or restore fellow church members who might fall into sin.

Any time a believer is not walking by the Spirit, that in itself means he is caught in a trespass. "Caught in any trespass" contains the idea of falling into a sin and becoming trapped or bound by it. Paul's use of "any" is notable because it won't let us make the excuse that some sins can't or shouldn't be confronted within our local churches. Every time we know of another brother or sister ensnared by sin, the Spirit wants us to act and seek his or her restoration.

The apostle is not saying that only those who are "super spiritual" or perfect can reach out to restore another believer. "You who are spiritual" simply means those who are being faithful to walk by the

Spirit, are thinking spiritual thoughts, and are letting the Word of Christ dwell richly within their hearts and minds. In 1 Thessalonians 5:14, Paul in similar fashion urged mature Christians to minister to weak and sinning believers: "We urge you, brethren, admonish the unruly, encourage the fainthearted, help the weak, be patient with everyone." And this sort of exhortation is not merely something that was distinctive with Paul. He was just being faithful to expand upon the basic teaching of the Lord Jesus, who provided the precedent for a ministry of restoration among believers with His teaching on church discipline in Matthew 18:15–17 (see also 5:23–24).

Paul told the Galatians and us very clearly in Galatians 6:1 how we should go about the process of picking up a brother or sister who has stumbled: "Restore such a one in a spirit of gentleness." The Greek verb for "restore" is in the continuous present tense, which suggests that we will likely have to use a patient, persevering process whenever dealing with another Christian in need. The process involves essentially repairing (as in mending fishing nets) or setting something straight (as in realigning a frame or some joints). These definitions ought to demolish any persistent notion that confrontation and restoration within local churches are optional ministries.

If we rely on the wisdom and guidance of the Holy Spirit, we will restore another believer with gentleness. A kind and gentle manner should be automatic for us, because one aspect of spiritual fruit is gentleness (Gal. 5:23). However, the ideal of what ought to be does not always match the reality of what is. Hence, we need Paul's reminders in Galatians 6 and elsewhere on how to deal rightly with sinning brethren within the church (see 2 Cor. 2:7–8; 2 Thess. 3:15).

Bear One Another Up

No one can doubt that sincere, godly love has an extremely high priority in Scripture, and thus within God's plans and purposes. It is certainly one of the attributes of God, and it was one of the divine motivations and initiatives behind His plan of salvation (John 3:16; Rom. 5:8). The Lord Jesus said love is the defining mark of believers: "A new commandment I give to you, that you love one another, even as I have loved you, that you also love one another. By this all men will know that you are My disciples, if you have love for one another" (John 13:34–35). Our Lord also set forth two aspects of love as the summary elements of the entire law of God: "He said to him, '"You shall love the Lord your God with all your heart, and with all your soul, and with all your mind." This is the great and foremost commandment. The second is like it, "You shall love your neighbor as yourself." On these two commandments depend the whole Law and the Prophets'" (Matt. 22:37–40).

It logically follows, then, that love will be a characteristic attitude and action of any believer who walks by the Spirit. Love is closely connected with how such a believer will minister to other Christians, as Galatians 6:2 shows us: "Bear one another's burdens, and thereby fulfill the law of Christ." When we get involved with others and help them hold up their particular burdens, we are obeying the law of love. James called it "the royal law" (James 2:8), and it is the second aspect of spiritual ministry to one another.

On the surface, the phrase "bear one another's burdens" is concise but rather open-ended. What exactly does it mean to bear another person's burden? Commentator William Hendriksen shared these relevant insights:

> This does not merely mean "Tolerate each other," or "Put up with each other." It means "Jointly shoulder each member's burdens." Everybody should put his shoulder under the burdens under which this or that individual member is groaning, whatever these burdens may be. They must be carried jointly. Though the term "one another's burdens" is very general, and applies to every type of oppressing affliction that is capable of being shared by the brotherhood, it should be borne in mind, nevertheless, that the point of departure for this exhortation … is the duty to extend help to the brother so that he may overcome his spiritual weaknesses.[6]

Even though "burden" can apply to many different obligations, difficulties, and sins, the Greek term means an excessively heavy, unbearable load, which one person alone can't carry. This fact drives home the point once again that in the body of Christ we need each other. The Holy Spirit is concerned about each member and wants to use each of us to give mutual support.

Earlier in our study we saw that Hebrews 10:23–25 clearly implies that it's neither good nor in God's will for Christians to attempt to "go it alone." One of the major reasons, which all of us could verify simply from past experience, is that it is much harder to resist temptation to sin when we are by ourselves for any length of time. A persistent, oppressive, heavy burden of temptation will become unbearable with no one alongside to help, and we will inevitably fall, perhaps repeatedly. On the other hand, we have all noticed how when we are regularly among other believers in a sound church with strong fellowship and teaching, the strength and accountability of those spiritual friendships help maintain our walk in the Spirit.

Spiritual responsibility to one another is really what burden bearing is all about, and we can accomplish it in very practical ways. One is to arrange for regular times to talk together about spiritual issues. You can hold the other person accountable during those times by having him or her report how things are going with regard to a certain temptation, bad habit, or tough challenge. You can also pray for the person regularly and check with him or her to see how those prayers are being answered.

In summary, the scriptural ministry of bearing burdens entails much more than just confronting someone about a certain sin and then walking away (see James 2:16–17). It actually involves a reciprocal building process in which we and the other person together benefit from God's truth. As Paul said in Galatians 6:6, "The one who is taught the word is to share all good things with the one who teaches him." This process wonderfully blends together, thanks to the presence, indwelling, and guidance of the Holy Spirit, our Silent Shepherd, who exhorts and instructs through us and grants us the privilege of walking with Him.

Walking in the Spirit is not complex, mystical, or reserved for an elite minority of saints. Thus, we don't need secret knowledge, manipulative techniques, creative gimmicks, or special experiences. Instead, the entire pattern for walking spiritually is linked to the basics of Christian discipleship, which all believers can glean from

Scripture. The key is nothing more nor less than spiritual vigilance and daily perseverance. That's why Paul wrote, "Be on the alert, stand firm in the faith, act like men, be strong. Let all that you do be done in love" (1 Cor. 16:13–14).

8

REALIZING OUR FULL POTENTIAL—IN THE SPIRIT

Sometimes an easy conversation between friends can have ramifications far beyond what either person expects. Such was the case in the summer of 1872 near Dublin, Ireland, when two prominent evangelists were conversing about ministry. The two men were British evangelist Henry Varley and renowned American evangelist Dwight L. Moody. Their conversation contains one of the best-remembered quotes attributed to the life and times of Moody. The remark affected him for the rest of his life.

The morning after an all-night prayer meeting, as the two men strolled around the grounds of the mansion where the meeting had been held, Varley uttered a brief but thought-provoking statement to Moody. This is how it was recorded in one of Moody's diaries:

> "The world has yet to see what God can do with and for and through a man who is fully and wholly consecrated to Him." ... A man! Varley meant *any* man. Varley didn't say he had to be educated, or brilliant, or anything else. Just a *man*. Well, by the Holy Spirit in me I'll be that man [italics mine].[1]

Henry Varley's words became indelibly fixed in Dwight Moody's heart and mind and were a tremendous motivation for the gifted American evangelist's final quarter century of ministry. A short while after his walk with Varley, Moody was further impressed by the need to be completely obedient to the Lord:

> Back in London, in the gallery of the Metropolitan Tabernacle, Varley's remark and Spurgeon's preaching focused Moody's attention on "something I had never realized before. It was not Spurgeon who was doing the work: it was God. And if God could use Spurgeon, why should He not use me?"[2]

If one Christian's informal remarks to another believer—especially to one who was already a prominent leader—could stir that individual's thinking so much regarding sanctification and effective service, the words ought also to stir believers like us. This episode from the life of Moody encourages us to wrestle with the issue of what it means to be empowered by the Holy Spirit. A proper way to do that is to consider this final question: What does it mean to be filled with the Spirit?

God's Command to "Be Filled"

Ephesians 5:18 contains this imperative from the apostle Paul: "Be filled with the Spirit." This concise, straightforward injunction is loaded with significance for believers. However, that significance is often misunderstood, misapplied, or missed altogether. To begin with, many Christians are unclear about what the verse does not mean. Once we discard the incorrect meanings, we can then focus on what Paul was really saying.

Wrong Equations for Filling

First, this phrase is not commanding empty Christians to acquire something they don't already have. Each of us, as we saw earlier in our study, possesses the entire Holy Spirit from the time we repent and believe (see again Rom. 8:9–10).

Second, Paul's phrase is not equating fullness of the Spirit with baptism with the Spirit. Holy Spirit baptism is not an extra experience that we need to seek; it is something we have from the moment we are saved. This baptism is a theological reality, an act by which Jesus Christ through the agency of the Spirit places us into the body of Christ (1 Cor. 12:13; see also John 7:37–39).

The Right Equation for Filling

An understanding of the Greek word for "be filled," *plerousthe*, quite clearly reveals the correct meaning of Paul's command in Ephesians 5:18. A literal translation of the verb would read something like "be being kept filled." The idea is one of keeping ourselves constantly filled, as we yield moment by moment to the leading of the Spirit. It fits perfectly with the process of walking by the Spirit.

An accurate rendering of the Greek verb also destroys the widespread charismatic notion that being filled is a onetime emotional experience we initiate, which instantly places us into some inner circle of spiritual maturity. "Be filled" is actually in the passive voice and indicates that we receive the action—the Holy Spirit is continuously filling us. It is simply another facet of the Spirit's indwelling ministry, which allows us to have daily, moment-by-moment effectiveness and fulfillment in our Christian lives.

Facets of Spiritual Filling

When we use the word *fill* in English, we normally think of something being placed into a container such as milk being poured to the brim of a glass, water being run into a bathtub, or gasoline being pumped into a gas tank. But none of those examples conveys precisely the meaning of *to fill* or *be filled* as does the Greek *pleroo*, a form of which is used in Ephesians 5:18.

Pleroo has three shades of meaning that are helpful in illustrating the scriptural meaning of Spirit-filled. The first carries the idea of pressure. It is used to describe wind billowing the sails on a ship, providing the impetus to move the vessel across the water. In the spiritual realm, this concept depicts the Holy Spirit providing the thrust to move the believer down the pathway of obedience. Spirit-filled Christians are not motivated by their own desires or wills to progress. Instead, they allow the Holy Spirit to carry them in the proper directions. Another helpful example of this first meaning is a small stick floating in a stream. Sometime in our lives most of us have tossed a stick into a creek and then run downstream to see the twig come floating by, propelled only by the force of the water. To be filled with the Spirit means to be carried along by the gracious pressure of the Holy Spirit.

Pleroo can also convey the idea of permeation. The well-known pain reliever Alka-Seltzer illustrates this principle quite effectively. When one or two tablets are dropped into a glass of water, they instantly begin to fizzle and dissolve. Soon the tablets have been transformed into clear bubbles throughout the glass, and the water is permeated with the distinct flavor of the Alka-Seltzer. In a similar sense, God wants the Holy Spirit to permeate and flavor our lives so that when we're around others, they will know for certain that we possess the pervasive savor of the Spirit.

There is a third meaning of *pleroo*, actually the primary one in the New Testament, which conveys the sense of domination or total control. The gospel writers used the term in various passages to indicate that people were dominated by a certain emotion. In Luke 5:26, after Jesus rebuked the Pharisees and healed the paralytic, the people were astonished and "filled with fear." In Luke 6:11, when Jesus restored a man's hand on the Sabbath, the scribes and Pharisees "were filled with rage." When our Lord told the disciples that He would soon be leaving them, He told of their reaction: "Sorrow has filled your heart" (John 16:6). Each of those uses reveals an emotion so overwhelming within the people that it dominated their thoughts and excluded every other emotion.

Most people are able to balance their emotions throughout their lives. But there are some occasions when the emotional balance is tipped to one extreme or another. Such occasions include one's wedding, the death of a close family member, or a stressful emergency or trial. When someone is totally dominated by a particular emotional reaction in secular contexts, it can be foolish, a waste of time, or even frightening and harmful. But in our spiritual lives we are commanded to yield to the total control of the Holy Spirit, so that every emotion, thought, and act of the will is under His direction. This kind of complete spiritual control is for our benefit and totally in line with God's will.

There is a directly parallel passage in Colossians 3:16, which equates exactly with the Ephesians 5:18 command to "be filled with the Spirit." The apostle Paul expressed the very same truth with these words: "Let the word of Christ richly dwell within you." One can be filled with the Spirit only when controlled by the Word. It is knowing truth and obeying it.

Practical Consequences of Being Spirit-Filled

The apostle Paul followed up his inspired command that we be filled with the Spirit by attesting to what will be evident in our lives if we genuinely obey that exhortation:

> Speaking to one another in psalms and hymns and spiritual songs, singing and making melody with your heart to the Lord; always giving thanks for all things in the name of our Lord Jesus Christ to God, even the Father; and be subject to one another in the fear of Christ. (Eph. 5:19–21)

Paul's statement outlining the results of being filled with the Holy Spirit provides us with an appropriate capstone to our extended study of the person and ministry of the Holy Spirit. Now that we have dealt with the meaning of the divine command to be filled with the Spirit, having already considered His various indwelling works on our behalf and our ample resources for walking in Him, you may quite fairly be asking, "How can I really know if I'm walking in step with the Spirit and realizing His fullness?" The apostle answers this with three clear evidences for judging the Holy Spirit's full operation in our lives.

Singing to the Lord

The place of music and singing in the church and the Christian life could be the topic for a separate book, and of course skilled and godly musicians have written various volumes about all aspects of music. So there are helpful resources for us to refer to on this subject. However, I think many of us might still approach Ephesians 5:19 wondering just how the matter of singing relates so directly to the great doctrinal truth of verse 18. But there is a relationship—the first consequence of being Spirit-filled is that we will have a song in our hearts—and other Scripture passages will help us understand it.

Evangelist Billy Graham once wrote this about the role of song in the believer's life:

> God put a song into man, but sin garbled it, distorted it, and brought discord into his life. When a person repents and puts his trust unreservedly in Jesus Christ, God gives him back the melody that was almost muted. That is the secret of the Christian life.[3]

The Bible is silent on the pre-fall role music and song had, but we can safely infer that music has been important to humankind from the earliest times (see Gen. 4:21). Moses and the people of Israel praised God after they were delivered from the Egyptians (Ex. 15). Likewise, Deborah and Barak sang following their victory over Sisera (Judg. 5). And of course the Psalms are filled with references to song, music, and praise, culminating in this exhortation in the very last verse of the book: "Let everything that has breath praise the LORD. Praise the LORD!" (Ps. 150:6).

Other references in the New Testament are also significant in their mention of song. Jesus and His disciples sang a hymn at the close of the Last Supper (Matt. 26:30; Mark 14:26). Believers in the early church were probably singing their prayer in Acts 4:24–30, and Paul and Silas definitely were singing as they sat chained in the Philippian dungeon (Acts 16:25). Paul lifted up singing in Colossians 3:16, the parallel passage to Ephesians 5:19 (see also James 5:13). Finally, in the last book of the New Testament, the apostle John made this prominent reference to song:

> When He [Christ, the Lamb] had taken the book, the four living creatures and the twenty-four elders fell down before the Lamb, each one holding a harp and golden bowls full of incense, which are the prayers of the saints. And they sang a new song, saying, "Worthy are You to take the book and to break its seals; for You were slain, and purchased for God with Your blood men from every tribe and tongue and people and nation. You have

> made them to be a kingdom and priests to our God; and they will reign upon the earth." Then I looked, and I heard the voice of many angels around the throne and the living creatures and the elders; and the number of them was myriads of myriads, and thousands of thousands, saying with a loud voice, "Worthy is the Lamb that was slain to receive power and riches and wisdom and might and honor and glory and blessing." And every created thing which is in heaven and on the earth and under the earth and on the sea, and all things in them, I heard saying, "To Him who sits on the throne, and to the Lamb, be blessing and honor and glory and dominion forever and ever." And the four living creatures kept saying, "Amen." And the elders fell down and worshiped. (Rev. 5:8–14; see also 14:3; 15:3–4)

This is not just any song being sung before the throne of God, as the words themselves make plain. The song is so special that John called it a "new song," which in the Greek means not merely a new song chronologically, but a new one qualitatively. Every time this Greek term for *new* is used in the New Testament, it is in connection with salvation. So it is logical that those who are saved and filled with the Holy Spirit will sing a new song, one that is radically different from the world's songs. If there is anything tangibly new in the Christian life, it ought to be the songs that rise from our hearts during worship services and other gatherings. Such songs are the products of the Holy Spirit, who indwells us and causes us to break forth in praise because of the joy we have in submitting to Him.

Giving Thanks to the Lord

Ephesians 5:20 gives us a second virtue that will result when a believer is truly filled with the Spirit: The believer will be thankful toward God. I have long been convinced that gratitude is the single greatest act of personal worship we can render to God. William Hendriksen lent support to this contention: "The expression of gratitude is therefore a most blessed response to favors undeserved. While it lasts, worries tend to disappear, complaints vanish, courage to face the future is increased, virtuous resolutions are formed, peace is experienced, and God is glorified."[4] Genuine thankfulness also sees beyond the difficult or baffling circumstance to the sovereign plan and purpose of God (see Rom. 8:28–29).

Always

The apostle Paul made it clear to the Ephesians that thankfulness is to be a well-rounded, complete response that affects all areas of life. First, the Spirit-filled person will be *thankful always and at all times.* In Ephesians and elsewhere Paul made it crystal clear that this is the Lord's will for us: "In everything give thanks; for this is God's will for you in Christ Jesus" (1 Thess. 5:18; see also Eph. 5:17; James 1:25).

Such a consistent, no-exceptions-permitted reaction to what the Lord brings into our lives is not easy or even possible in our own strength. But it will become our response all the time if we are living the Spirit-filled life. The Holy Spirit works graciously and mercifully to enable us to respond with thanksgiving no matter when blessings or challenges come. Sometimes He blesses us unexpectedly, which makes it easy to give thanks. The gratitude and praise of Moses and the Israelites after God delivered them by parting the Red Sea is one major example of that (Ex. 14—15).

At other times the Holy Spirit gives us the opportunity to be thankful before a certain event happens. If the anticipation is for something pleasant, like a vacation or reunion with a loved one, thankfulness is again easy for us to display. But if the anticipation is more difficult or frightening, then it becomes a test of our faith. In 2 Chronicles 20, King Jehoshaphat and his people passed this test prior to a battle against the Ammonites and Moabites. When it was reported to him that a large army was coming against Judah, Jehoshaphat immediately asked the Lord for help. The Spirit of the Lord then revealed His encouragement through the prophet Jahaziel, and the Levites and all the people worshipped and thanked God prior to their success against the enemy (2 Chron. 20:1–23).

Finally, God may choose to bring a trial or test into our lives more unexpectedly. Then we'll be challenged to give thanks in the midst of the battle, when it is the most difficult to respond righteously. Jonah, in spite of all his sinful shortcomings, presents us with an excellent example of just such a right response. After the giant fish swallowed him, Jonah prayed this to the Lord: "While I was fainting away, I remembered the LORD, and my prayer came to You, into Your holy temple. Those who regard vain idols forsake their faithfulness, but I will sacrifice to You with the voice of thanksgiving. That which I have vowed I will pay. Salvation is from the LORD" (Jonah 2:7–9). God honored Jonah's prayer and delivered him from the fish, right to the location he was supposed to be. We may never be as severely tried as Jonah was, but God in His providence may allow unexpected hardships. If we respond with true thanks in the midst of such times, that will prove we are mature Christians who are filled with the Spirit.

For All Things

If the Spirit-filled believer is thankful at all times, it reasonably follows that he or she will also be *thankful for all things*. We have just seen that difficult times will also include difficult matters for which we must give thanks (see again James 1:25; see also Heb. 12:3–13; 1 Peter 2:20–21). But we could also enumerate dozens of positive things that Scripture reminds us to be thankful for. Some of the major ones include: the goodness and mercy of God (Pss. 106:1; 107:1; 136:1–3), the gift of Christ (2 Cor. 9:15), the triumph of the gospel (2 Cor. 2:14), victory over death and the grave (1 Cor. 15:57), the reception and effectual working of God's Word in others (1 Thess. 2:13; 3:9), and the supply of our bodily wants (Rom. 14:6–7; 1 Tim. 4:3–4). Each of those categories contains many more specific items for which we can be grateful, so the point is that those filled by the Spirit know no limits or distinctions on what to thank God for.

In the Name of Christ

Finally, those who are filled with the Spirit will give thanks *in the name of Christ to God the Father*. This means, first of all, that we couldn't be thankful at all if it weren't for Jesus Christ and what He has done for us. "In the name of Christ" simply means being consistent with His character and His deeds. An excerpt from Paul's awe-inspiring opening chapter to the Ephesians summarizes this concept very well:

> He predestined us to adoption as sons through Jesus Christ to Himself, according to the kind intention of His will, to the praise of the glory of His grace, which He freely bestowed on us in the Beloved. In Him we have redemption through His blood, the forgiveness of our trespasses, according to the riches of His grace which He lavished on us. In all wisdom and insight … also we have obtained an inheritance, having been predestined according to His purpose who works all things after the counsel of His will, to the end that we who were the first to hope in Christ would be to the praise of His glory. (Eph. 1:5–8, 11–12)

No matter what happens to us, we can give thanks because of what Jesus means to us, and we can know that because of God's sovereignty, whatever happens to us will turn out for our good and His glory.

The object of Spirit-filled thanksgiving is God the Father. This name for God emphasizes His loving benevolence toward His children and the constant stream of gifts that flow to us from His all-powerful hands. James 1:17 reminds us of this: "Every good thing given and every perfect gift is from above, coming down from the Father of lights, with whom there is no variation or shifting shadow." If the apostle James was right, and he is, it is hard to imagine how believers could ever fail to give all their thanks to God. Long before either James or Paul instructed Christians about thankfulness, the psalmist did so many times to God's people (e.g., Pss. 30; 50; 69; 92; 95; 98; 100; 105; 118). There is just no escaping the importance of believers' continuously giving thanks to God at all times, for all things. The letter to the Hebrews offers this fitting capstone to our discussion: "Through Him then, let us continually offer up a sacrifice of praise to God, that is, the fruit of lips that give thanks to His name" (Heb. 13:15).

Submitting to One Another

The third practical consequence of being filled with the Holy Spirit is mutual submission to other believers: "and be subject to one another in the fear of Christ" (Eph. 5:21). Once again we have an aspect of the Spirit-filled life that reflects and draws together a principle that is found many other places in Scripture. Since we have already dealt with issues related to mutual submission earlier in this book, I'll address the matter here only briefly.

The Bible is replete with statements and exhortations about the importance of being subject to one another and ministering to one another. I want to highlight some and list various others to underscore the importance the Holy Spirit has given to the concept of believers supporting one another.

Romans 12:5 says, "So we, who are many, are one body in Christ, and individually members one of another" (see also Acts 2:44; 1 Cor. 12:12; Eph. 2:11–22). Romans 14:13 says this regarding the relationship of weaker and stronger brethren to one another: "Therefore let us not judge one another anymore, but rather determine this—not to put an obstacle or a stumbling block in a brother's way" (see also 1 Cor. 8). Ephesians 4:11–12 tells of the major spiritual gifts that build up the church: "And He gave some as apostles, and some as prophets, and some as evangelists, and some as pastors and teachers, for the equipping of the saints for the work of service, to the building up of the body of Christ" (see also 1 Cor. 12:8–10). First John 4:7 has this basic command about love for one another: "Beloved, let us love one another, for love is from God; and everyone who loves is born of God and knows God" (see also John 13:34–35; Eph. 4:2; Col. 3:14; 1 Thess. 3:12; 1 Peter 1:22; 1 John 2:10; 4:11). Philippians 2:3–4 is a classic passage on regarding the interests and welfare of others: "Do nothing from selfishness or empty conceit, but with humility of mind regard one another as more important than yourselves; do not merely look out for your own personal interests, but also for the interests of others" (see also Rom. 12:10; 1 Cor. 4:7; 1 Tim. 5:21; James 2:1). Hebrews 13:17 gives believers important guidance concerning submission to spiritual leaders: "Obey your leaders and submit to them, for they keep watch over your souls as those who will give an account. Let them do this with joy and not with grief, for this would be unprofitable for you" (see also 1 Thess. 5:12–13; 1 Peter 5:5).

All of those traits and actions, and many more in the New Testament, are parts of the normal, submissive lifestyle of the Spirit-filled Christian. The word *submission* from the world's perspective has the connotation of weakness or caving in to a much stronger, overbearing authority. But that is not what it means biblically. Martyn Lloyd-Jones put the correct connotation and meaning into perspective:

> It is the picture of soldiers in a regiment, soldiers in a line under an officer. The characteristic of a man in that position is this, that he is in a sense no longer an individual; he is now a member of a regiment; and all of them together are listening to the commands and the instructions which the officer is issuing to them. When a man joins the army he is as it were signing away his right to determine his own life and activity. That is an essential part of his contract. When he joins the army or air force or the navy, or whatever it is, he no longer governs and controls himself; he has to do what he is told. He cannot go on a holiday when he likes, he cannot get up at the hour in the morning when he likes. He is a man under authority, and the rules dictate to him; and if he begins to act on his own, and independently of the others, he is guilty of insubordination and will be punished accordingly. Such is the word the Apostle uses; so what he is saying amounts to this—that we who are filled with the Spirit are to behave voluntarily in that way with respect to one another. We are members of the same regiment, we are units in this same great army. We are to do that voluntarily which the soldier is "forced" to do.[5]

The only way to voluntarily and joyfully submit to the Lord and to one another in the body of Christ is to be filled with the Spirit. He is the one who truly makes us willing to follow the narrow path of submission and relinquish our wills for His. I sincerely trust that by now, at the end of this study, you have a much clearer, more focused idea of what that voluntary submission and obedience is. It is nothing else than the way of Christian discipleship and sanctification. It is available to all who repent, believe in the saving work of Christ, and receive the Holy Spirit, our Silent Shepherd.

Knowing that Shepherd is really much the same as knowing Jesus, the Good Shepherd. It is not something reserved for the preacher, the theologian, the missionary, or any elite spiritual group. Receiving the Spirit, walking by the Spirit, and living in the fullness of the Spirit are not magical, mystical things, obtained only by some supercharged emotional appeal to a "second blessing." Instead, the presence and aid of the Spirit are simply aspects of the Christian life, which God makes available in abundant measure to all believers. Our task is, through prayer, study of Scripture, fellowship, and all the other means of grace, to realize these great truths and to persevere by the Spirit's power moment by moment, step by step, in living them out. May God help us all to know the full presence and ministry of the Holy Spirit, the Silent Shepherd in our lives (Jude vv. 20–21).

DISCUSSION GUIDE

For Personal Study

Settle into your favorite chair with your Bible, a pen or pencil, and this book. Read a chapter, marking portions that seem significant to you. Write in the margins. Note where you agree, disagree, or question the author. Look at the relevant Scripture passages. Then turn to the questions listed in this study guide. If you want to trace your progress with a written record, use a notebook to record your answers, thoughts, feelings, and further questions. Refer to the text and to the Scriptures as you allow the questions to enlarge your thinking. And pray. Ask God to give you a discerning mind for truth, an active concern for others, and a greater love for Him.

For Group Study

Plan ahead. Before meeting with your group, read and mark the chapter as if you were preparing for personal study. Glance through the questions, making mental notes of how you might contribute to your group's discussion. Bring a Bible and the text to your meeting.

Arrange an environment that promotes discussion. Comfortable chairs arranged in a casual circle invite people to talk with one another. Then say, "We are here to listen and respond to one another—and to learn together." If you are the leader, simply be sure to sit where you can have eye contact with each person.

Promptness counts. Time is as valuable to many people as money. If the group runs late (because of a late start), these people will feel as robbed as if you had picked their pockets. So, unless you have a mutual agreement, begin and end on time.

Involve everyone. Group learning works best if everyone participates more or less equally. If you are a natural talker, pause before you enter the conversation. Then ask a quiet person what he or she thinks. If you are a natural listener, don't hesitate to jump into the discussion. Others will benefit from your thoughts—but only if you speak them. If you are the leader, be careful not to dominate the session. Of course, you will have thought about the study ahead of time, but don't assume that people are present just to hear you, as flattering as that may feel. Instead, help group members to make their own discoveries. Ask the questions, but insert your own ideas only as they are needed to fill gaps.

Pace the study. The questions for each session are designed to last about one hour. Early questions form the framework for later discussion, so don't rush by so quickly that you miss a valuable foundation. Later questions, however, often speak of the here and now. So don't dawdle so long at the beginning that you leave no time to "get personal." While the leader must take responsibility for timing the flow of questions, it is the job of each person in the group to assist in keeping the study moving at an even pace.

Pray for one another—together or alone. Then watch God's hand at work in all of your lives.

Notice that each session includes the following features:

Session Topic—a brief statement summarizing the session.

Community Builder—an activity to get acquainted with the session topic and/or with one another.

Group Discovery Questions—a list of questions to encourage discovery and application.

Prayer Focus—suggestions for turning one's learning into prayer.

Optional Activities—supplemental ideas that will enhance the study.

Assignment—activities or preparation to complete prior to the next session.

1

THE SILENT SHEPHERD: A PRIMER

Session Topic

The Holy Spirit is the third person of the Trinity and has definite roles and representations, which Scripture spells out.

Community Builder (Choose One)

1. What significance have you attached to the Holy Spirit in your previous studies of God's Word? During your experience in church and with other fellowship groups?

2. Have you ever bought something that needed a good owner's manual or instruction booklet, but was without one? How frustrating was that? Recall a specific example if you can.

Group Discovery Questions

1. What does the Apostles' Creed say about the Holy Spirit? Are you surprised that this creed does not discuss Him in more detail? Why or why not?

2. Other books on the Holy Spirit usually discuss Him from one of two basic approaches. What are these?

3. What truth does the quote from T. S. Caulley convey? How would you summarize this in your own words?

4. Why is it important to understand that the Holy Spirit is a person?

5. What three major personal attributes of the Spirit are mentioned in this chapter? How does Scripture, both Old and New Testaments, support these?

6. What is an *anthropopathism*? Why is this figure of speech helpful in our study of the Holy Spirit?

7. Name four truths about the Holy Spirit's activities that demonstrate His personhood. Which one gives the most convincing proof that the Spirit has a personality?

8. Which other persons does Scripture say the Holy Spirit has a relationship with? What does this imply about the Holy Spirit's dealings with us?

9. What attributes of God does the Holy Spirit also possess? Name at least three of the ones listed in this chapter.

10. Why is it evident that the Spirit's three major works show His deity? What are these important works?

11. What are four of the Silent Shepherd's other works that benefit us? What is the more specific expression for these operations?

12. Name three of the symbolic representations the New Testament uses for the Holy Spirit. Include one that is less familiar or less frequently used. How are these symbols helpful?

Prayer Focus

- Thank God that the Holy Spirit is not a mere force or influence but is the third person of the Trinity.

- As you continue this study, ask the Lord to grant you a clearer perspective on all the aspects of the Holy Spirit's being and ministry. Pray that God would give you and your group a scripturally balanced appreciation for the role of the Silent Shepherd.

Optional Activities

1. Do some additional reading on the doctrine of the Holy Spirit. Read appropriate sections from a good systematic theology (e.g., Charles Hodge or Louis Berkhof). Or you may want to obtain a copy of Paul Enns's *Moody Handbook of Theology* (1989) and read chapter 21.

2. Read Romans 8:1–30 several times next week. Notice how often this passage mentions the Holy Spirit. In what ways is the Spirit involved in our Christian life? Make a brief list or outline of these.

Assignment

1. Memorize John 14:16–18.

2. Read chapter 2 of *The Silent Shepherd.*

2

THE SPIRIT IN THE OLD TESTAMENT

Session Topic

Whether during the old or new covenant era, the same Holy Spirit ministers to believers in the same basic ways.

Community Builder (Choose One)

1. Was there ever a time when you really failed to communicate accurately an important concept? If so, what kind of difficulty and embarrassment did the miscommunication create?

2. Share an experience from school or work in which you sensed the special empowerment from God's Spirit to

accomplish a challenging or complex task. Could you have mastered the situation without the Spirit's help?

Group Discovery Questions

1. What did Paul say about the similarity between the Spirit's role in the Old Testament and His role in the New? Support your answer with at least one Scripture reference.

2. How may the meaning of the Genesis phrase "moving over the surface of the waters" be illustrated?

3. Why did Jesus reprimand Nicodemus in John 3:5–10? What does that passage show us about how the Holy Spirit works?

4. What is the definition of spiritual empowerment in the Old Testament? Whom did the Holy Spirit empower during that period?

5. What did the judges do in Israel? Why was that action so important for the nation?

6. What was the first important, large-scale project of craftsmanship accomplished by those who were empowered by the Holy Spirit?

7. Does the withdrawal of the Spirit's empowerment remove the eternal security of believers? Why or why not?

8. What does 2 Timothy 3:16 say about the Spirit's work in revealing God's Word?

9. How early in the Bible did the Holy Spirit convict humankind of sin?

10. Other than forgiveness of sins, what crucial need does David's prayer in Psalm 51 reveal?

Prayer Focus

- Ask the Lord to give you a greater desire to study and understand the Old Testament.

- Spend some time praising and thanking God for His Spirit's sustaining presence in creation.

- Thank God for the special gifts and abilities He's given you. Pray for wisdom to use these for His glory.

Optional Activities

1. Begin a reading program in some portion of the Old Testament, such as the prophets (Isaiah) or the historical books (Joshua). If you are already doing this, choose one book for more detailed study.

2. Write a note or letter of thanksgiving and encouragement to one of the leaders in your church. If possible, mention something specific the leader has done recently that's been a blessing to you.

Assignment

1. Memorize 1 Corinthians 12:13 or Ephesians 4:4.

2. Read chapter 3 of *The Silent Shepherd.*

3

THE SPIRIT OF LIFE: THE NEW COVENANT

Session Topic

The new covenant, as a better covenant than the old, gives us a fuller manifestation of the Holy Spirit.

Community Builder (Choose One)

1. Is something new always an improvement over the old version? Why or why not? Share some specific examples.
2. Have you ever rewritten a contract between yourself and another party? What sorts of things in the contract did you retain? What other elements of it did you seek to improve?

Group Discovery Questions

1. When did Jesus first tell His disciples there would be a new covenant? What did His own words say about the basis and purpose of that covenant?

2. What is a mediator? What is necessary for a mediator's work to be most effective?

3. Who were the mediators under the old covenant?

4. Give at least three ways in which the new covenant is different from and better than the old. What is the most important feature that is the same?

5. Of the seven superior new covenant characteristics in Hebrews 8:8–12, which ones do you believe should have the greatest impact in believers' lives? Why?

6. What place do the Ten Commandments occupy in the thinking of most Christians? How familiar do you think the average believer is with what each commandment actually says?

7. Why do some assert that Christians are free from the moral law's requirements? What did the apostle Paul really say in Romans 6 about the law?

8. What has happened to the place and purpose of the civil and ceremonial laws?

9. What is a good, basic definition of the moral law? What gospel passage provides a good summary of the moral law?

10. What are the three purposes for the moral law?

11. What place should the moral law have in your life today? Reread the long quotation from Martyn Lloyd-Jones on this topic. How is his summary helpful?

12. How does Paul's reference to Moses' glowing face (Ex. 34) illustrate the contrast between the covenants? (See 2 Cor. 3:7–11.)

Prayer Focus

- Spend some extra time in prayer to thank God for giving us the new covenant. Thank Him specifically for each feature.

- Reflect on one or more of the Ten Commandments that are especially challenging for you to obey. Ask the Lord to strengthen you as you seek to be more faithful in these areas.

- Ask the Lord to grant you a better understanding of and appreciation for the contrast between the old and new covenants. Thank Him for the privilege of being able to live under the greater glory and fuller revelation of the new.

Optional Activities

1. Obtain a copy of a good catechism, such as the "Westminster Shorter Catechism," and study the section on the Ten Commandments over the next month. Write out and meditate on answers and Scripture verses that are most helpful to you.

2. Over the next several months, work on memorizing Exodus 20:2–17. Divide the passage among five or six index cards and work through the cards one at a time as you learn the entire passage.

Assignment

1. Memorize Matthew 26:27–28.

2. Read chapter 4 of *The Silent Shepherd.*

4

THE SPIRIT OF TRANSFORMATION AND HOPE

Session Topic

The new covenant is the Christ-centered covenant that transforms us and provides life and hope.

Community Builder (Choose One)

1. What was your sense of hope like prior to salvation? Was it absent or just focused in the wrong place? Explain.

2. Most of us have certain daily rituals or routines that are important to us. What is one of yours? Could this become a snare that would hinder your spiritual walk?

Group Discovery Questions

1. How did Paul use the term *letter of the law* in reference to the old covenant law?

2. How did the letter create a living death for Paul?

3. What is the curse referred to in Galatians 3:10? What is the only way to escape the effects of this curse?

4. Why can ceremonialism be harmful to someone's spiritual welfare? How did it affect the Jews?

5. Why and how is the new covenant permanent? What comfort does that permanency bring to those who embrace the new covenant?

6. What human response caused the old covenant to be viewed with such lack of clarity? How was such a response illustrated on the road to Emmaus? (See Luke 24:13–32.)

7. What event most vividly demonstrated Christ's divine glory to Peter, James, and John? (See Luke 9:28–36; 2 Peter 1:16–18.)

8. What is new covenant hope? How did the apostle Paul present it in Romans 8:23–25? What piece of maritime equipment does Hebrews figuratively equate with hope?

9. "The Ugly Duckling" is a familiar and beloved fable, but what does it illustrate about the new covenant?

10. What New Testament verse best affirms and illustrates the change the Holy Spirit works in the believer's life?

Prayer Focus

- Think of a friend, relative, or coworker who does not know Christ. Pray each day next week that he or she will come to enjoy the transforming power of the new covenant.

- Thank the Lord that the message of the new covenant is clear and Christ-centered. Ask Him to help you remove anything that may be clouding your view of Christ.

Optional Activities

1. Read the story of the ugly duckling to your children and explain to them how it illustrates the transforming power of the gospel. If you have no children, or yours are older, perhaps you could share the illustration with someone else's children.

2. If you have a Christian friend or family member who is now facing a trial or struggling with doubt, write him

or her a letter of encouragement. Share some of the key verses from this chapter.

Assignment

1. Read Hebrews 8:6–13 about the better covenant. Look up the Old Testament references quoted and read them in their original contexts.

2. Read chapter 5 of *The Silent Shepherd.*

5

THE PROMISED SPIRIT: A COMPLETE ARRIVAL

Session Topic

Jesus' promise to send the Holy Spirit has been completely fulfilled for all true Christians.

Community Builder (Choose One)

1. Recall something special that was promised to you as a child. How excited were you about it? Was the promise fulfilled, and was it as good as you expected it to be?

2. In the past, have you had a positive or negative opinion toward the expression "baptism of the Holy Spirit"? After studying this chapter, has your viewpoint changed?

Group Discovery Questions

1. When did Jesus first outline for His disciples the promise of sending the Holy Spirit?

2. What were some of the major evidences that Jesus' ministry was empowered and guided by the Holy Spirit?

3. Why would the Pharisees come to the conclusion they did regarding Jesus' ministry? Is their attitude still strong today?

4. Especially in older books, the Spirit is sometimes called the Paraclete. Where did this term originate and what does it mean?

5. How important is the Holy Spirit as a teacher for us? What happens when we ignore His instructions and operate in our own wisdom?

6. How is the peace that Jesus, via the Spirit, promises in John 14:27 different from the peace of Romans 5:1–11? How is it similar to the peace mentioned in Philippians 4:7?

7. What factor is most crucial to our full enjoyment of Jesus' supernatural promises? What is the key to having this element in our lives?

8. According to Acts 2:33, what is God's perspective on the promised Holy Spirit? What confidence should this give us?

9. How did Jesus illustrate the disciples' need to rely on supernatural empowerment for the most ordinary everyday tasks? In what specific way could you apply this to your daily responsibilities?

10. What is the best way for the average Bible student to read and understand the Acts 2:1–4 passage about Pentecost?

11. Why did God choose to have the outpouring of the Holy Spirit coincide with the Feast of Pentecost?

12. What was the real significance of the physical phenomena that accompanied the Holy Spirit's arrival in Acts 2? What further reassurances should this understanding give believers regarding God's sovereign plan?

13. What working relationship do Christ and the Holy Spirit have concerning Spirit baptism? (See Mark 1:7–8; John 7:37–39; Acts 2:32–33.)

Prayer Focus

- Pray together as a group and thank God that He fulfilled His promise to pour out the Spirit on Pentecost.

- Ask the Lord to solidify your understanding of the biblical meaning of Spirit baptism. Pray that His church would have greater clarity and unity on this matter.

- If you have a Christian friend who is striving to realize the American dream more than to appreciate the Holy Spirit's presence, pray for that person to have a change of heart.

Optional Activities

1. Read chapters 8 and 10 of my book *Charismatic Chaos* for additional insight into other interpretations of Acts 2. Write down your comments and questions and bring some of these up for group discussion at a subsequent meeting.

2. Read Acts 1—2 in at least three modern Bible translations (e.g., *New American Standard, New International Version, New English Bible*). Refer to a map in the back of your Bible or in a Bible atlas to locate the places in Acts

2:9–11. If you have time, look up the Old Testament references in Peter's sermon. Summarize in your own words the thrust of these two chapters in Acts.

Assignment

1. Memorize Romans 11:32–36 or John 7:37–39.

2. Read chapter 6 of *The Silent Shepherd.*

6

THE SILENT SHEPHERD AT WORK FOR US

Session Topic

The Holy Spirit gives us our true identity in Christ and enables us to know our benefits and obligations under the new covenant.

Community Builder (Choose One)

1. Talk about the various ways people try to find their identity in the world. Why do some of these avenues have such appeal?

2. Do you consider yourself an individualist or more of a team player? Explain how you think this answer affects your relationship to the Holy Spirit.

Group Discovery Questions

1. What is the most basic work the Holy Spirit performs on behalf of any individual?

2. What evidences coincide with a person's transformed life in the Spirit? (See Gal. 5:22–23.)

3. According to Romans 8:9, what establishes our spiritual identity?

4. Have you ever paused to take a spiritual self-inventory? (See 2 Cor. 13:5.) What are some basic questions you need to ask yourself?

5. Why do we share personal testimonies with other people? How does this parallel what the Spirit does? (See John 15:26; 16:14–15; 1 Cor. 12:3.)

6. Do you sometimes find it difficult to be sure of God's will regarding certain decisions? What principle do you find in Acts 15:28–29 about proper discernment of God's will?

7. How important is consistency in church attendance and involvement in smaller fellowship groups? What benefits

will we miss if we are not faithful in meeting with fellow Christians? (See Eph. 4:12; Heb. 10:23–25.)

8. What are spiritual gifts? What is the purpose for them and what ought to be our underlying attitude as we use them? (See 1 Cor. 12:7–11; 13.)

9. What does Ephesians 3:20 indicate about the extent of the Holy Spirit's power and His supply of strength available to us?

10. How do Christ's and the Spirit's intercessions on our behalf work together to preserve us as believers? What are the "groanings" referred to in Romans 8:26?

Prayer Focus

- Thank the Lord for graciously sending His Spirit to free us from sin and enable us to fulfill the law's demands.
- Has your love for Christ grown faint amid the stress and hectic pace of your daily schedule? Spend some additional prayer time asking God that His Spirit would direct your attention in a renewed way to Christ's glories.

- Pray that God would keep you alert and sensitive to the spiritual needs of others. Ask Him to give you an opportunity to minister to the specific hurt or struggle of someone in your church.

Optional Activities

1. Older hymns about the Holy Spirit are often overlooked, or Christians are unaware that many of them exist. Read and reflect on the lyrics of a few older hymns in a good hymnal (not just a chorus book). Write out one or two stanzas to meditate on and perhaps memorize.

2. Read 1 Corinthians 12 and 13. Write down the spiritual gift or gifts the Lord has given you. On the same piece of paper or card list two or three principles from chapter 13 that you especially need to work on as you use your gift(s). Carry this reminder in your Bible for future reference.

Assignment

1. Memorize Galatians 5:16 in preparation for your next meeting.

2. Read chapter 7 of *The Silent Shepherd.*

7

A SCRIPTURAL PATH FOR THE SPIRITUAL WALK

Session Topic

God's Word gives us all the direction we need to submit moment by moment to the Holy Spirit's leading.

Community Builder (Choose One)

1. In what area of life are you most prone to taking matters into your own hands and doing things your way? Why is that true? Can you recall a time when this approach especially caused a problem for you or others?

2. What are some ways you have dealt with distracting or daydreaming thoughts during a worship service or Sunday school class? Which methods seemed most effective in redirecting your attention?

Group Discovery Questions

1. What bearing does the story of Jacob and Esau have on our study of walking by the Spirit? What further insight does Hebrews 12:15–17 give concerning Esau's behavior?

2. How does understanding the Greek word for "walk" in Galatians 5:16 help us better to apply the verse?

3. In what ways is meditation superior to other means of Scripture intake? (Look again at the quotation from Donald Whitney's book.)

4. What important spiritual discipline will help us focus our hearts and minds on God?

5. What does 1 Thessalonians 5:17 say about the indispensability of prayer?

6. What does 1 Peter 2:11 say in the New King James Bible? How might this wording give us a better understanding of the nature of the spiritual walk?

7. What effect does our Western culture and lifestyle have on our ministry to one another? Have you noticed this affecting your own outreach to fellow believers? How?

8. What does the phrase "caught in any trespass" in Galatians 6:1 convey about the nature of sin? Is it all right to exclude any problem area from our ministry of restoration?

9. What will be the defining trait of believers no matter where they are? (See John 13:34–35.)

10. Although the term "burden" in Galatians 6:2 can mean a variety of things, what basic meaning characterizes all the usages?

Prayer Focus

- Ask God to help you live one day at a time and walk by His Spirit.
- Thank God for the bounty of spiritual food found in Scripture. Ask Him for a greater measure of diligence in daily reading of and meditating upon His Word.
- Pray that each person in your group would have a genuine desire to shun the flesh and submit to the Spirit in dealing with every aspect of their lives.

Optional Activities

1. Read John Bunyan's classic of the Christian life *The Pilgrim's Progress*. Keep a notebook of your most significant thoughts, impressions, and ideas for personal application.

2. Phone an out-of-town Christian friend whom you haven't been in touch with for a long while. If the person shares a special burden with you, assure your friend that you are praying for him or her. Follow up by mailing your friend appropriate literature and finding out what progress he or she has or has not made. Stay in contact and record the eventual results in a notebook or prayer journal. Even if things are well with your friend, you can encourage him or her with a verse or two of Scripture from this chapter.

Assignment

1. Memorize Galatians 6:2 or 1 Thessalonians 5:14.

2. Read chapter 8 of *The Silent Shepherd.*

8

REALIZING OUR FULL POTENTIAL—IN THE SPIRIT

Session Topic

The fullness of the Holy Spirit is a continuing facet of His indwelling, which allows believers moment-by-moment effectiveness in living for Christ.

Community Builder (Choose One)

1. Do you think most people reach their full potentials at work, with their families, at church? Why or why not?

2. Name one thing in your life over the past five years for which it was hard to give thanks. What's one thing for which it was easy to be grateful?

Group Discovery Questions

1. What were Henry Varley's words to Dwight L. Moody? How does Varley's statement challenge you?

2. What are two incorrect understandings of the Pauline command in Ephesians 5:18 to be Spirit-filled?

3. What literal translation did we suggest for *be filled*? What is the main idea it conveys regarding the process of walking by the Spirit?

4. Briefly review the three shades of meaning for *fill* in Greek. Which one helped you best understand the scriptural meaning of being Spirit-filled?

5. What are some important references to praise and song in Scripture? Give two Old Testament and three New Testament references.

6. In what way is the song in Revelation 5:8–14 "new"? How does this idea of new relate to the Christian life?

7. How may the timing of events in our lives affect the ease with which we are able to give thanks? (Look again at the examples of Jehoshaphat and Jonah.)

8. What are three significant truths for which Scripture reminds us to thank God?

9. What does "in the name of Christ" mean? How does this relate to the idea of giving thanks?

10. Which of the various "one another" passages quoted toward the end of this chapter is referred to as a "classic passage" on the topic of mutual submission?

11. As illustrated by Dr. Martyn Lloyd-Jones, what is the accurate, biblical connotation of the word *submission*?

Prayer Focus

- During the next several weeks in your prayer times, focus on what it means to be Spirit-filled. Ask the Lord to remove anything from your life that would keep you from being completely filled with His Spirit.

- Pray that God would help you be more aware of the practical consequences of the Spirit-filled life. Ask Him for the wisdom to apply specific aspects of these to your life.

- Thank the Lord for the time your group has spent studying the Holy Spirit. Pray that each member would be faithful to the Spirit-filled life in the months to come.

Optional Activities

1. Compile a list of things for which you can thank God right now. Add to the list over the next six months. Be sure to write down everything the Lord lets you experience, both pleasant and difficult. Review your list after six months and thank God for what He has taught you.

2. Take extra time one week to evaluate what you hear in Christian music. Listen to your local Christian radio station and some of your own purchased music. Write a critique of some of the songs: Are they "new songs" that reflect the fullness of the Holy Spirit? Do the lyrics have substance that is drawn from Scripture truths? How do the melodies compare with secular music? Is there a mix of contemporary music with the more traditional? In your evaluation, include the music from several services at your church. After reading chapter 8 of *The Silent Shepherd*, what grade would you give the music you heard?

Assignment

1. Finish one of the Scripture memory assignments that you began earlier in the study.
2. Lend *The Silent Shepherd* to a Christian friend or family member and ask for the person's feedback when he or she has finished reading the book.

NOTES

Introduction

1. Charles C. Ryrie, *The Holy Spirit* (Chicago: Moody, 1965), 9.

Chapter 1: The Silent Shepherd: A Primer

1. T. S. Caulley, "Holy Spirit," in *Evangelical Dictionary of Theology*, ed. Walter A. Elwell (Grand Rapids, MI: Baker, 1984), 527.

Chapter 2: The Spirit in the Old Testament

1. Edward J. Young, *In the Beginning: Genesis Chapters 1 to 3 and the Authority of Scripture* (Edinburgh, United Kingdom: Banner of Truth, 1976), 37.
2. George Smeaton, *The Doctrine of the Holy Spirit* (Edinburgh, United Kingdom: Banner of Truth, 1974), 23.
3. Ibid.

4. A. Lamorte and G. F. Hawthorne, "Prophecy, Prophet," in *The Evangelical Dictionary of Theology*, ed. Walter A. Elwell (Grand Rapids, MI: Baker, 1984), 886.
5. F. F. Bruce, *The Epistle to the Hebrews*, New International Commentary on the New Testament (Grand Rapids, MI: Eerdmans, 1964), 2–3.
6. J. I. Packer, "Regeneration," in *Evangelical Dictionary of Theology*, ed. Walter A. Elwell (Grand Rapids, MI: Baker, 1984), 925.

Chapter 3: The Spirit of Life: The New Covenant

1. Francis Turretin, *Institutes of Elenctic Theology*, 3 vols. (Phillipsburg, NJ: Presbyterian & Reformed, 1992), 2:145.
2. D. Martyn Lloyd-Jones, *Studies in the Sermon on the Mount*, 2 vols. (Grand Rapids, MI: Eerdmans, 1959), 1:195.

Chapter 5: The Promised Spirit: A Complete Arrival

1. Hezekiah Harvey, *The Pastor* (Rochester, NY: Backus, 1982 reprint), 164.
2. For more details regarding the meaning and timing of the day of Pentecost, see *The MacArthur New Testament Commentary: Acts 1—12* (Chicago: Moody, 1994), 39–40.
3. See my *Charismatic Chaos* (Grand Rapids, MI: Zondervan, 1992) and *The MacArthur New Testament Commentary: Acts 1—12* and *1 Corinthians*.
4. J. I. Packer, *Keep in Step with the Spirit* (Old Tappan, NJ: Revell, 1984), 89.

Chapter 6: The Silent Shepherd at Work for Us

1. Leon Morris, *The Gospel According to John*, New International Commentary on the New Testament (Grand Rapids, MI: Eerdmans, 1971), 90–91.

2. John Murray, "The Epistle to the Romans," vol. 1, chapters 1–8, *New International Commentary on the New Testament* (Grand Rapids, MI: Eerdmans, 1959), 313.

3. Arthur W. Pink, *Gleanings from Paul* (Chicago: Moody, 1967), 168.

Chapter 7: A Scriptural Path for the Spiritual Walk

1. For a detailed look at the conflict and contrast between the flesh and Spirit in Galatians 5, see my *MacArthur New Testament Commentary: Galatians* (Chicago: Moody, 1987), chapters 15–16.

2. Donald S. Whitney, *Spiritual Disciplines for the Christian Life* (Colorado Springs: NavPress, 1991), 44.

3. Dan DeHaan, *The God You Can Know* (Chicago: Moody, 1982), 17.

4. For a complete study of the nature and importance of prayer, see my book *Alone with God*.

5. Cameron V. Thompson, *Master Secrets of Prayer* (Lincoln, NE: Good News Broadcasting, 1959), 12–13.

6. William Hendriksen, *New Testament Commentary: Galatians* (Edinburgh, United Kingdom: Banner of Truth, 1968), 232–33.

Chapter 8: Realizing Our Full Potential—in the Spirit

1. Quoted in John Pollock, *Moody: The Biography* (Chicago: Moody, 1983), 115.

2. Ibid.

3. Billy Graham, *Crusader Hymns*, special Crusade edition (Chicago: Hope Publishing, 1966), preface.

4. William Hendriksen, *New Testament Commentary: Ephesians* (Edinburgh, United Kingdom: Banner of Truth, 1967), 241.

5. D. Martyn Lloyd-Jones, *Life in the Spirit: in Marriage, Home & Work. An Exposition of Ephesians 5:18 to 6:9* (Grand Rapids, MI: Baker, 1975 reprint), 57–58.